Seven Dragons:

a guide to a limitless mind

To Joe, Jason and Julia

"You are the heart of my life."

I would like to thank some of my teachers
and mentors along the way:

Bob Proctor, Wayne Dyer, Caroline Myss,
Maxwell Maltz, Abraham-Hicks, Michael Gerber,
Jack Canfield and Baron Baptiste.

Contents

Preface

"Believe nothing. No matter where you read it, or who said it, even if I have said it, unless it agrees with your own reason and your own common sense."
~Buddha

TIME TO FLY. It's all because you had a dream and other people told you it was out of reach. It's time to let go of the past, tone your wings, feel the fire and tap into your divine potential.

Wake up! This is your life! This is self-coach guide that challenges you to go beyond your natural limits. Here's the jump off! Are you ready?

"Promise Yourself...

To be so strong that nothing can disturb your peace of mind.

To talk health, happiness, and prosperity to every person you meet.

To make all your friends feel that there is something worthwhile in them.

To look at the sunny side of everything and make your optimism come true.

To think only of the best, to work only for the best and to expect only the best.

To be just as enthusiastic about the success of others as you are about your own.

To forget the mistakes of the past and press on to the greater achievements of the future.

To wear a cheerful expression at all times and give a smile to every living creature you meet.

To give so much time to improving yourself that you have no time to criticize others.

To be too large for worry, too noble for anger, too strong for fear, and too happy to permit the presence of trouble.

To think well of yourself and to proclaim this fact to the world, not in loud word, but in great deeds.

To live in the faith that the whole world is on your side, so long as you are true to the best that is in you."

~ Christian Larson, The Optimist's Creed

Words of Caution

Some lessons in this book may not align with your current perspectives and beliefs. My father always says, "We can disagree and not be disagreeable." So, if something doesn't feel right to you, that's okay – don't believe it. I have written the lessons, tips, and tools that have been explained to me by many well known success experts. These lessons have made such a profound impact on my life that I could help but offer them as a gift to you.

Many lessons in this book may seem so simplistic and you may neglect to put them in practice. Reading is only the first step to learning, integrating, and believing. You must journal, practice and take action on these principles.

Introduction

> *"Be still like a mountain and flow like a great river."*
> ~Lao-Tse

You are about to understand how, as a spiritual being, you can change your mindset to experience phenomenal success and authentic truth. You will learn how to create and design a life without struggle or stress and live a life of flow.

As you read this book, you will also need a journal or notebook. Journaling and logging information offers an experimental and systematic approach to lifestyle design.

We have been taught to hide from or attack our problems instead of looking to our highest self for direction. We spend too much time on the small details of daily life and not enough time looking at our future vision and inner viewpoint. This step-by-step, hand-holding guide will help you design the life you desire, rewire your mind and surrender to your highest self.

I spent much of my late teens and early adulthood in a state of anxiety and depression. It seemed as if I was always chasing something, trying to get something or being someone else or somewhere else. Eventually, I did get what I desired, whatever it was that I was chasing. Family members would point out I was lucky, or that I could turn any bag of thorns into a bouquet of roses. Yet, I still wasn't happy. There were moments of exhilaration when I knew I was going to get what I had been working for, but there was little true happiness.

In 1997, I began to practice yoga regularly at a local gym. I started attending class during work lunch breaks. Hah, I had used yoga mostly as a way to take longer lunch breaks and escape the daily grind. For me, the hardest part of yoga was final rest (savasana). Now, I know that it was difficult because on some level, I feared knowing myself on a deeper level. I didn't really like myself.

I was afraid of my other self? Who was this other self? I am just one person. Aren't I?

I realized yoga had become an escape from my dual self. Or should I say my dueling self? Yoga was escape from this "other" voice, this negative self-defeating voice in my head. Hah, while other people choose the use of drugs or alcohol, not me, I chose yoga as my drug of choice. Thankfully, it has awakened me to a life of inspiration, consciousness, and flow.

By 2005, I chose to end my corporate career. By the time I left, I was miserable yet still felt trapped by a high paying salary and absolutely zero respect whatsoever. I was tortured with thoughts, "How could I possibly leave such a high paying job? I can't make this kind of money doing anything else." Boy, was I wrong! Who was I to tell myself this?

I told myself, "I can't." No one who loved me would tell me such nonsense, whether they thought it or not. Where did I get such ideas? Maybe I didn't love myself. At a minimum, I was verbally abusive to myself. Who had I become? I, of course, didn't realize this until much later. And then magic started to happen.

One Saturday in March of 2005, I received a phone call from a man in Arizona. At the time we didn't have a cable phone or caller ID or who knows if I would have even answered the line. My number was not available online or in the phone book. The man asked if there was a person who practiced transcendental meditation in our home. I said, "No, but I am very spiritual and I practice and teach yoga." He then, asked if it was Kundalini yoga and again I said, "No. I practice Vinyasa and Astanga yoga." I was starting to get a little defensive and agitated with his questions. Who was this guy and was he questioning me? I began thinking that it was some kind of joke or perhaps he had found my name on some yoga list. Finally, I asked who he was and why he was calling. He said he was a TMer. At the time, I had no idea what a TMer was. He explained that TM stands for Transcendental Meditation. It's not a religion or philosophy and it can be practiced by anyone looking to experience more mental clarity or reduce stress. I understood it as a form of meditation, but nothing more. He told me that during meditation he saw my number and had a strong sense that I needed to know that the universe was in support of my new direction.

The next week I spent a week practicing yoga at a spiritual retreat center. After each day of practice we journaled on our experiences. After a few hours of intense yoga we would journal about a given topic or our "after-yoga" thoughts. My journal entries included random statements such as... "We die in the comfort zone. Step out of your comfort zone. There is peace with truth. There is no peace with self-doubt. Life is full of options. We must have the courage to face the truth." I remember crying because at the time I wasn't following my true path and I felt miserable because of it.

The Monday after the retreat, I wandered back into my corporate office refreshed and relaxed. Then I thought, "What am I doing here? Is this just a pay check for me?" I knew a job like mine was a dream job for others, but why couldn't I just be thankful for what I had? I made it through the day and cried to my husband about my miserable job that night. He had some inspiring wisdom. He asked, "How will your life change if you leave this job? My job will support our current living patterns until you get up to speed with your own business. You will still have your computer, cable T.V. and your car. Your life won't change. I want you to be happy." It seemed so simple to him, but to me it was huge.

By the end of the day on Tuesday, my hard drive crashed. No, not the hard drive of my brain, but my computer's hard drive. I would joke to co-workers, "Do you think God is telling me something?" Many would just giggle, but one man said very seriously, "Yes! You have all this talent waiting to be let out. Jen, what are you doing here? What are you waiting for?" These words stuck with me. What was I waiting for? Why was I holding on to a job that I disliked? Why was I torturing myself?

My new computer wasn't delivered until the following Friday. The computer company didn't even try to recover my hard drive. What had taken them so long? Those three days of workless suffering brought me to the conclusion that I had to quit. That day, on my new computer, I wrote up my resignation letter.

Like all life journeys you must start with awareness and the basic understanding of what "Lifestyle Design" means. Patanjali wrote, "When you are inspired by some great purpose, some extraordinary project, all your thoughts break their bonds; your mind transcends limitations, your consciousness expands in every direction, and you find yourself in a new, great and wonderful world." For me, 'Lifestyle Design' means simply living your dreams at peace without resistance, fear, stress, struggle or strife.

The following chapters provide a collection of mindset 'reset' success tools to enable you to live your life with ease, flow, and extraordinary success. Throughout this book, I offer Dragon Diary Entries and strategies to tame your dragon-like mind. No matter how simple they seem, please don't discard them.

If practiced with discipline, the information in this book will transform your life.

Your Successful Future

The most common misconception about lifestyle design (life success) is that it is believed to exist in the future or that it isn't possible to achieve.

You don't have to go find your true self because you aren't lost. You may be hidden under limiting thoughts and ideas, but you are not lost. You were born a genius, complete with an abundance of resources.

As an emotional eating life coach, I found that many clients were crippled by the fear of weight gain, overeating, or just plain disordered eating behaviors. I started to teach them tools to become more focused and present, allowing them to overcome their fear and increase their self-esteem. With these tools, they learned how to love and honor their physical form, so they could live in the moment and reduce/remove the stress of not having the physical body they desired.

Living in the moment helped them let go of primal subconscious addictions. The word addiction alone demonstrates how we identify with behavioral patterns. You can't be addicted to something by using it one time in the 'now' moment. You have to have a habitual pattern of use to be addicted.

My work didn't stop there, I helped my clients discover and fill unmet needs, so they could feel more fulfilled and complete. This included self-coaching practices and tools that taught self-love, acceptance, and comfort. These practices and tools helped them change and/or even discontinue their disordered patterns. Many of them had labeled themselves as overeaters, emotional eaters, anorexic or bulimic, but on-the-road to recovery. Once they could accept that they had made eating mistakes in the past and could empower themselves to leave it in the past, they were open to a whole new set of beliefs. They could leave the 'label' behind and get on with their lives with more ease.

Please note: This book is not about coping habits; it's about transforming your mind. Many of my clients had seen previous counselors who had taught them methods to cope with their habits. This is not about coping! I want to teach you something much greater: How to completely transform your way of thinking.

Learning conscious presence gave them the opportunity to accept themselves today. Their inner agony faded whether their physical body was thinner or not. They no longer felt they had to suffer and strive for a better body, instead they embrace themselves and only addressed the food or exercise in the "now" moment.

The Secret Is Hidden Inside Your Dragon-like Mind

One of my clients was a multi-millionaire; she told me that 80-90% of her financial success was due to her faith and confidence. Imagine, 90% due to her mindset!

This got the wheels in my mind turning. Hmmm... so the other 10% was knowledge, while 90% was mindset/internal patterns? I began to play with the mindset of success. When I say, "play," I mean extreme study. How can you get the success you want in life? I have narrowed the path down to 10 rules! Ah, yes, more rules to live by. Fit these into your life and let go of the limiting rules.

Rule #1. Indulge Your Fantasy. Learn how to open your mind to a new set of ideas, perceptions, fantasies and beliefs.

Rule #2: Know Yourself: Know who you are,

what you clearly desire, and how to live 'on-purpose'.

Rule #3.   Have Pure Energy: Enhance your mental and physical energy. Attract opportunities like a magnet

Rule #4.   Be Inspired: What is inspired and what is a need-driven desire?

Rule #5.   Empower Yourself: Empower yourself with the choices you make and the people and environments you have chosen.

Rule #6.   Know Your Dragons: Knowing your dragons means understanding how the dragons in your mind might be working against you or holding you back from getting what you desire.

Rule #7.   Reset Your Mindset: Retraining your dragons teaches tips, tools, and strategies on how to reset your mindset

Rule #8:   Be Fabulous: When you are fabulous, do fabulous things and have fabulousness, you can't help but honor and celebrate yourself each day, everyday!

Rule #9.   Have Faith: When we operate from a place of faith, we have wings to fly beyond what we know.

Rule #10.   Invoke Your Intuition: Develop your intuition and use your inner intelligence to guide you.

Reminder: Like most things worth learning and doing, this, too, requires patience, practice, and persistence.

Bring a Journal On Your Discovery Journey!

Your journey is about to get a little sweeter. Bookmark this page and locate a journal to accompany this book. A journal will be needed for daily dragon discoveries, reminders, and action steps. I call it a Dragon Diary!

Got it? Great! Let's get started.

Rule #1:
Indulge Your Fantasy

> "Anything that you can imagine
> is yours to be or do or have."
> ~ Abraham-Hicks

WHAT'S YOUR EXCUSE? What's getting in your way of achieving your dreams? Could it be you – the perceptions you have created in your mind? That's right! The way you think, perceive and respond to everything! Your mind can change your life from a so-so life to the phenomenal life you have only dreamed about!

Why do some people find extreme success while others seem

to struggle to pay their bills each month? Is it intelligence, luck, or chance? The universe operates in a very orderly way. Doesn't it? Things don't happen by chance. We see this through everyday astrology and science. The universe was created in divine synchronistic order and has two objectives: to love and grow.

What is an opened mind? I see it as an opened door to a dragon dungeon, a.k.a., mind. The door is opened in order to allow new information to get in and limiting patterns and beliefs that aren't serving you to escape.

You have just brewed a cup of tea and have found a comfy chair. You crack this book open and begin. Now, Look up. There's your fairy godmother appearing in front of you. She offers you three minutes to answer this question, "What do you desire?" she asks. What do you say? Do you have a vision of what your future life looks like?

Dragon Diary Entry

It's time to answer your fairy godmother's questions... What do you desire for your life? Not what "stuff" do you desire, but what experiences, interconnections, and feelings do you desire? You may want to start with a list of what you LOVE doing. Include as many details you have available to you. Complete this question, not only for your life, but for your business or work, as well. Don't skip this step! I'll say it again, please don't skip this step! If you want to read on, please make a note to come back to this step. Or better yet, complete the book and address these journal entries on your second read.

Okay. Now, you have an idea of what you desire. Create your dream day, dream job, a dream vacation. Here are some questions to get you started. You wake up and feel ____ covers, pillows, love etc. You step on the scale and see ___. You have ___ for breakfast. You get in ____ car and feel ____. You love ___. I think you get the idea.

To indulge your fantasy further, go back to your dreams and desires you have just written and write down

(cont.)

the reason <u>WHY</u> you desire these life experiences on this trip to earth. Hmmmm... Why do you want this big house? How will that make you feel? What is it that you really want? The big house? Or the feeling of living in your big house? It could be the feelings of recognition, accomplishment, or luxury. What is your trigger? Is it an inspired desire? Or are you trying to fill some unmet need?

Okay. One more question to answer. What if you <u>HAD</u> to manifest your desires? What action steps would you take?

The Perfect Day – written by Bill Schneider, financial advisor:

I wake up at around 6am, completely refreshed and rejuvenated; I am grateful. I am in our $5,000,000 home on Makena Beach in Maui, Hawaii. I am awakened by the lips of my wife's soft, subtle good-morning kiss. Our Shih-Tzu, Mia; our Maltese, Hana; and our Yorkie, Ella are all cuddled up together at the bottom of the bed; they are also awakening, and you can hear their little grunts as they yawn and stretch their sleepy legs... The silk drapes are gently swept by the crisp south-pacific breeze. I feel the soft, gentle caress of our 1000 thread-count sheets, and the

mattress and pillows support my body and my
head as if I had just spent the night in the worlds
finest five-diamond resort; I can hear the whales
outside our bedroom window, singing their sweet
orchestral tune... a tune composed in heaven,
manifested just for me on this day. The smell of
the salt-water air is refreshing; it's as if, with each
breath I am given new life... a fresh, new breath,
which equals a fresh, new beginning today. I sit
up in bed and stretch my arms... the sun gently
cascades across the room, kissing the contours
of my wife's face... we say nothing, yet with one
gentle, pure gaze into one another's eyes nothing
is un-said.

My feet touch the bamboo floor; I shout a whisper
to God, "thank you..." I grab my soft, fluffy white
robe and wrap my body in it, heading downstairs
to watch the sunrise on our private lanai',
overlooking turtle-bay: an area of the pacific
where the turtles congregate while the whales
inhabit the deeper waters of the pacific. "I am so
happy and grateful," I exclaim, once again, with
the silence of my heart... I stand at the edge of
the lanai, which overlooks a rocky cliff; the sun
is now gently peaking over the mountains in the
horizon. I hold my cup of coffee in my hand, as
if to warm my hands, and take in the delicious
smell of the freshly ground Kona beans; my wife,
also in her white-fluffy robe, gives me a securing
hug from behind, gently laying her head on my
shoulder- she whispers, 'I love you...' "is this
heaven, I wonder?"

I shower in our marble/granite, custom-made
shower with twelve showerheads; the water

pours over me, gently sweeping away any cares
I might have begun this day with; the eucalyptus
soap and shampoo causes me to slip into an
intoxicating state of the senses... As I exit the
shower I reach for my towel, which is draped over
a rare sterling silver towel rack, which I obtained
from a visit to Tokyo just a few years earlier...
I pass through my den to get to my closet; on the
desk rests a bank statement... once again, this
time out loud, I say, "Thank you, God..." it's hard
not to get choked up as I continue to absorb the
beauty and greatness around me: my beautiful
wife; our beautiful home on the ocean; our babies
(the doggies)... everything we have... I have,
ever dreamed of had come true...

I enter my closet, where there resides thirty of
the finest pieces of clothing ever created by man,
and for that matter ever known to man: ten
Oxford suits, ten Ravazzolo suits, and nine Brioni
suits, and one Brioni Tuxedo; I have an extensive
collection of Farragamo shoes, belts, and bill-
folds; I reach in a drawer to put on a watch... I
have Fifty of the absolute finest time-pieces at my
discretion: which includes an extensive collection
of Genuine Panerai, Patek-Phillipe, Maurice
Lacroix, Corum, Baume and Mercier, and other
limited edition, very rare pieces such as a Genuine
Panerai 1950... I am so happy and grateful...

I enter the garage, but not before giving my wife
a squeeze and a gentle kiss and caress of the
cheek; she asks me to let go, and make it an
exceptional day...

I open the door to my silver Maserati Gran-

Turismo; I think to myself: "Man, I love that new car smell..." the supple red-leather seats invite me for the ride of my life... the engine sounds like the deep bellowing of a boxer's heart before a big fight... I exit our private, gated, drive and enjoy the acceleration of 604 horses galloping down the ocean's shoreway...

The Universal Law

Now, I want to introduce a few basic laws before we dive in and retrain your dragon-like mind. First, another word of caution: I often use the word "universe." If it feels right, you can translate the word to "God". This is a book about making your life and business flow with more ease--not a religious or spiritual book. However, since we are all spiritual beings, it is difficult to discard all spiritual information.

Here are a few universal laws to creating a life with more ease and flow.

Law #1:   Humbly and genuinely ASK for what you desire. Yes. If it feels right, get on your knees and pray.

Law #2:   LOVE yourself and everyone around you. This means to be grateful for everything and everyone you have in your life. Also forgive anyone you haven't forgiven already. I don't care how bad it was... forgive them. Don't give others the power to tax your energies. I want you to start whole and fresh!

Law #3:   KNOW (Believe) what you desire is coming your way. Knowing is a critical element that is often misunderstood and will be discussed later in the book. You must know without a shadow of a doubt that your desire will be manifested in your life.

Law #4:   ALLOW it into your life. Be resistant-free to the opportunities that come to you. (We'll talk more about the dragon a.k.a. habit of resistance later.)

We manifest every belief we have whether they are positive or negative. The universe is obedient and directs us to achieve the thoughts we choose or neglect to choose. If you believe it, the universe offers a direction for you to achieve it.

Degrees of Belief

In learning these basic universal laws, law #3 and #4

"Knowing and Allowing" were where I kept getting tripped up. You have to "BELIEVE" it! You have to "ALLOW" it! I found myself thinking... "OK. I get it. Yes. I believe it." What I found was that I understood the principles and felt as if I believed them, but my life still didn't seem to flow with ease.

Then, in a flash, my life changed when I started to KNOW what I desired was already available to me. I know it sounds strange, but this mindset changed the way I saw the world. Finally, I knew what I desired was available to me in the unmanifested form. It was in my mind. That's where it needed to be for me create it. I just needed to imprint it into my subconscious and unconscious mind then it would unfold naturally in the manifested physical world. I just needed to believe it was mine to create. When I felt what I desired was already available to me, things began to appear. In fact, I couldn't help it from unfolding. That's because my subconscious mind doesn't know the difference between what is non-physical and what is physical. This is why subliminal advertising is so effective -- it allows information to go directly to your subconscious mind so you will go manifest it. For example, at a movie you would go buy popcorn or a soda without any resistance to doing so.

Whatever it is, you need to KNOW you can create it. This takes care of both the believing and the allowing. When you

KNOW you can create something, you have faith and you aren't resistant to the small steps and leaps you have to take to get there.

Before we go on, I want to introduce what I call the five degrees of belief. These feelings offer insight to why things might not be flowing into your life. You may be feeling doubt. You could be 'doubting' these words you are reading. That's okay, but it won't make your life any simpler or flow better. This approach requires a different way of thinking and feeling.

The five degrees of belief are doubt, hope, understand, believe and know. They are all feelings that you can change. You have the choice to change these feelings.

What can you do to change your feelings and emotions?

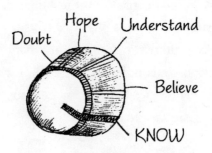

Can you change ... ***doubt --> into hope, hope --> into***

understand, understand --> into believe, and believe --> into KNOW?!

Let's explore how the different beliefs feel in the body. If you can get a good sense of how a belief feels then you have the power to deliberately change any thought and feeling if necessary. It's just a feeling after all. It's easy, as I go through each description, give it a try.

Let's start with 'DOUBT.' What does DOUBT feel like to you? Where do you feel it in your body? If you aren't making $100K per month now and I tell you can within 90 days. You may think, "Yeah, right." This is how if feels to 'DOUBT'. Please make note of how this feels. You may even want to put it in your journal.

Next there's 'HOPE.' Every week you play a local bingo game. It seems like you have a 50-50 chance of winning. You feel somewhat positive you may win this week. This is how 'HOPE' feels. You got it?

Now, 'UNDERSTAND.' Let's say your have been taught something, but have not yet experienced it to be true; you don't know 100%, but you could see how it could be true. Children naturally skip past understanding to believing. They don't have past experiences with which to compare their belief. They don't question. They just get on to believing what they are told whether the information is the truth or not. As adults we become more skeptical. We compare the new information with our current belief system and decide if the new information fits in. We do not ask if the information is the truth or if it will help us live more fulfilled lives. You may be doing this right now.

One day, I made $10,000 and I told my son, "Wow. I made $10,000 today." He said, "Well, someday you will be making a million." I automatically responded with, "Well, maybe not in one day." And then I caught myself. I don't need to be installing my limiting ideas into my offspring. In fact, I don't need to be installing such thoughts into my own mind.

This brings us right into 'BELIEVE.' When you experience something a few times, but don't always get 100% results. You BELIEVE you won't get a cold over the holidays. Can you know this to be a fact? If you said, "No," this is how it feels to BELIEVE.

> **If you think you can do a thing or you think you can't do a thing, you're right**
> ~ Henry Ford

Sometimes people confuse believing with knowing. I am

using the words we say. For example, "I BELIEVE I can run a half-marathon" is different than "I know I can run a half-marathon." In this case believing may mean I am not 100% sure since I might have to walk some of the way.

This brings us to 'KNOW', which is when you have experienced something to be 100% true. You KNOW you can swim three laps, balance on one foot for a three seconds or read a book. This is how it feels to KNOW.

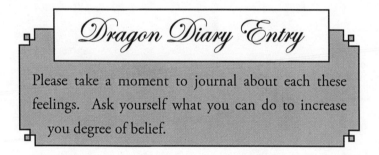

Dragon Diary Entry

Please take a moment to journal about each these feelings. Ask yourself what you can do to increase you degree of belief.

Rule #2:
Know Yourself

> "In every block of marble I see a statue as plain as though it stood before me, shaped and perfect in attitude and action. I have only to hew away the rough walls that imprison the lovely apparition to reveal it to the other eyes as mine see it."
> ~ Michelangelo

YOU: Y.our O.bjective in the U.niverse

WHO 'THE HECK' ARE YOU? What is your true nature?

I mean your raw true being before you were programmed with stories by your external world? We are on planet Earth to love, enjoy, share and create what we desire. When you feel blissful, you are on your divine path.

Dragon Diary Entry

Let's explore your divine path and potential. Review your earlier journal entries to see how your dreams are aligned with your feelings of love and joy. Is there something you desire that isn't included? What do you want to add or change?

Are Your Dragons Trapped in a Dungeon?

Do you feel trapped or in a rut? Doing the same 'ol, same 'ol? Maybe you don't know your divine path or potential? Or you don't feel that what you are doing is 'divine' enough. If you quilt, write novels, or repair cars, whatever it is, as long as you enjoy it then you are on your divine path.

If you aren't happy with what you are doing with your days, you may need to 'ASK' (Rule #1) for direction. Reading this book might be the first time you have even really thought about your path. My advice is for you to notice what makes you feel on fire or excited. It could be as simple as baking a dessert. Let your desires and feelings be your guide. Take Joseph Campbell's advice, "Follow your bliss." When you feel in love or bliss with what you are doing, you are on the right path and on-purpose. So, relax and follow your heart and your bliss.

Okay. Are you present and with me? Are you reading these words through your eyes? Have you written your ideas in your journal and noticed your bliss? Yes? Let's take this a step deeper.

Dragon Diary Entry

Title the next page and leave a couple of pages for a "What am I doing list?" This offers some insight into where you are spending your time.

Take this diary/journal everywhere with you for at least one week. Make a list of everything you do. No details needed. Just one line per item is fine, number them, and leave space for modification ideas.

For example:

    1. Take Susie to daycare

2. Check e-mail

3. Make cold calls

4. Take Susie to dance practice.

Make note of everything you don't want to be doing in your daily life. Next, put an 'X' next to the things you dislike and can remove from your daily list. Then put a ' * ' next to things you dislike but can't remove. Create a plan to either enjoy these activities or a plan to change the activities. Review your list to easily identify where you aren't following your divine path.

YOU: The Being

> "Were you only this body, you would have no news of the spirit"
> ~ Rumi

We are first and foremost spiritual beings. You just can't ignore this fact. You are that thing inside your body that hears with those physical ears and sees with those physical eyes. Because we are spiritual beings housed in a human body, we have both human and spiritual potential. That's why miracles show up all the time in our lives and others.

Y.O.U. = a spiritual being + a human physical form + mind (the connector between human, physical, and spirit).

MIND: Beyond The Brain

The brain has three main components that explain why we do the things we do.

1. The cerebral cortex
2. The limbic system
3. The brainstem

The cerebral cortex (conscious mind) is responsible for conscious thought. This includes reasoning, perceiving, image producing and understanding.

The limbic system (subconscious mind) is responsible for memory images, mental patterns, fight or flight responses and emotions, such as anger, fear, and pleasure.

The brainstem (unconscious mind) is responsible for basic living functions. This includes the heart, breathing, eating, and sleeping. The unconscious mind also offers an avenue for inspiration. When inspirational ideas come to us, they find us in the form of vibration through the unconscious mind.

When you observe the mind, you will find there are four processes to observe. (T.I.M.E.)

1. Thoughts (conscious)
2. Images (conscious and subconscious)
3. Mental Pattern or Behaviors (subconscious)
4. Emotions (subconscious)

The brain is the functioning physical tool that works with the mind. The brain is a part of the mind. The mind includes divine inspiration, intuition, sensory instincts and our sixth sense. The mind connects us to collective consciousness and unconsciousness. Or if you prefer... the mind connects us to spirit, God and the universe.

DRAGON MASTERS
Know the mind is apart of spirit.

Thoughts, images, mental patterns, emotions and feelings (T.I.M.E.) are energies and a part of the body, mind, and spirit network. All these mental processes transmit energetic vibrations. Although we cannot see them with our five senses, quantum physics have shown that they are vibrations and they emit at a very high frequency. In fact, Elisha Gray says in *The Miracles of Nature*, "Light and heat are manifested by vibrations of a far lower intensity than those of thought, but the difference is solely in the rate of vibration."

A Single Thought

Let's start with a single thought. Thoughts are in the conscious mind when we hear them. The conscious mind includes thoughts that you hear in your head, such as "Am I saying this out loud or in my head?" These internal thoughts are changeable.

Conscious thoughts are on two planes. The first plane includes the intelligent thoughts. It sometime says, "Hmmm... I wonder if Sheila will take Sammy to the park today? Maybe I'll give her a call." You hear these words in your head. This is an example of an inspired thought.

The second plane is the repeating mental retro records or mental chatter. It is just there. It doesn't usually make a lot of sense. Occasionally, you will catch it in the act when you get dressed in the morning, suddenly you may think, "Augh, I'm so fat." Or you'll look in the mirror and say, "I look old." These thoughts have been repeated so many times, you don't really notice them anymore. But these thoughts are our gateway to changing our subconscious and unconscious minds. Let's start paying attention to these thoughts. These engrained retro record-like thoughts are often small pieces of larger belief patterns. Luckily, they can be caught with these similar thoughts. In other words, pay attention to what you are saying to yourself. They can only be found when we observe our minds. When you find yourself saying, "I can't. It's difficult. I am not good enough." Change these thoughts immediately. Jot them down in your journal whenever you can. Awareness is the first step to changing and rewiring the mind.

Not all mental chatter is negative but it is still mental chatter and can be quieted, controlled and trained to come up when it is needed.

Take a deep breath.... ready for more?

This single conscious thought, whether deliberate, inspired or insipid, can lead to strong emotions, which can lead to another thought and even stronger emotions. It can go something like this.... someone complains in an e-mail to you, this causes you to think your work isn't good, this causes you to feel sad and unworthy, this emotional feeling can then trigger deeper depressive feelings from past unmet needs. This can go the other way too. Maybe your work was praised.

What series of emotions would you feel then?

When you feel emotionally charged (strong emotion) about a subject, the feeling is already housed in the subconscious mind. The subconscious mind is like a computer's hard drive. You were born with a clear open mind and over time you add information, which became mental patterns, beliefs, behaviors and habits as you experience life.

The truth is nobody can make you feel shame, guilt, apathy, grief, anger or even excitement. You must learn to take responsibly for how you CHOOSE to feel all the time. This doesn't mean to ignore or discard your feelings. It means choose to look on the bright side or the right side of things. We embody the laws of the universe when we exercise our power of choice. What's your next move? What's your next consequence? And what is the quality of the consequence when your mind is aligned with your intention?

Rule #3:
Have Pure Energy

"Somewhere in you there lies (sleeping), the seed of achievement, which if aroused and put into action, would carry you to heights, such as you may never have hoped to attain."
~Napoleon Hill

WHAT'S ALBERT EINSTEIN GOT TO DO WITH IT? In 1905, Albert Einstein rocked the scientific community with his proven theory of relativity: $e = mc^2$ his equation demonstrated that energy and matter are interchangeable. e represents energy. m represents mass while c^2 is the square root of the speed of light. This means energy and matter are essentially the same! We think of a desk or a chair as being solid, but they are really just a lot of atoms, bonds, and energetic space. Nothing is really solid. So what does this mean to your life and business? This means that your mental thought patterns are energy as well. This means that clutter, annoyances, and random unclear thoughts are getting in your way energetically. It's all just a bunch of atoms whizzing around distracting you from your purpose.

Your challenge is to align these atoms and get them pulling in the same direction. You can do this by only thinking and sending out thoughts of what you want in crystal-clear congruent messages and images. To become more naturally attractive and successful, you must get rid of all energy drains and add life, fun, excitement and energy back into your world.

When you experience a random thought here and a dab of mental chatter there, you have mental chaos! Mental chaos emotionally drains us. As a coach, I teach my clients how to take a hard look at what they are thinking and doing that may be causing them to feel drained and/or have mental chaos. What are you thinking and doing that may be causing mental chaos and draining your energy?

"Pure energy" is that feeling when you feel "on-fire" and "on-purpose" in every area of your life! You feel excitement, fun, laughter and even clarity! "Pure energy" is extremely powerful and makes you unstoppable.

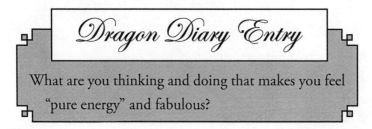

Space

Law of vacuum: When something departs from your reality, it creates a vacuum that can draw in something new and better, just as space does.

Have you ever heard that space abhors a vacuum? There is reason this phrase was created. By creating space, you naturally increase your ability to attract something new into your life. Have you ever noticed that when you empty a room or a drawer it doesn't stay that way for long? Have you noticed that when your house is clean you feel great? Yes? So you know it gives you energy.

The same is true with the mind. When you clear the cluttering thoughts in the mind, it allows more divine inspiration to flow in.

In the Bible, Jesus withdraws from the crowds or goes alone on tasks. These messages are indications that we need to get quiet and refuel our personal energy cup for clarity, concentration and focus.

Holding past emotional patterns in your mind lowers your natural energetic frequency and will cause you to manifest your desires at a slower rate. If you feel an energetic aliveness or "on-fire" feeling, you respond and take action. You feel this way when your mind is clear, focused and aligned with receiving your desires. You don't hesitate, ponder, procrastinate or resist decisions and actions. So wouldn't you naturally be manifesting at a faster rate? This means to stay focused on your passions and concentrate on making them a reality. This means stop holding emotions of regret, anger, rage, and worry and do what you need to do to make your dreams become a reality.

If you are holding on to mental attitudes, unfinished business, and other mental clutter how is it possible for God to get a word in? Mental energy tied up in past conversations, events, petty annoyances, and stories are constrained energy that you can't use in the present moment. This is literally emotional baggage. If each morning you were given 100% pure energy and you automatically had to put 50% into your past unfinished business that you wouldn't let go of, how much would you have left? That's right, 50% would be gone. You are putting your energy in past thought forms like anger, anxiety, and depression instead of positive, focused thoughts.

Many mindful practices, such as yoga, tai chi, and qigong suggest that you focus on the space between the sentences, the space between breaths, and to notice the space. I've heard suggestions like, "Notice how a room would be nothing without space." Why do you think that is? If you notice and give attention to space, you begin to create more mental space. What you give attention to will expand!

Can you wake up each morning feeling alive, refresh and new? When you complete pending tasks you begin to feel more energetic and complete. That is because your energy is literally weighed down and invested in physical and mental clutter. Any and every small annoyance is a tiny zap of energy. Some petty annoyances and tolerations can be as simple as rips in clothes that you can't wear, light bulbs that are burnt out and unflattering clothes. This may also include people that seem to be taking energy from you by their attitudes or behaviors. You know who they are.

Dragon Diary Entry

Make a ZAP List. This list includes all the petty annoyances, tolerations and other physical and non-physical clutter you could, should or would like to clean up in your life. What do you need to do to clean up your life? Why haven't you done it yet?

Below are three questions to ask yourself about physical and mental clutter.

1. Do I need to **take action** on this idea or thing? This can also include delegation. Do I need to give this to someone else to deal with?

2. Do I need to put it away for later or **file it**?

3. Do I need to **discard or let it go**?

Synchronicity

If 90-100% of your energy (or pure energy) is in present time – synchronicity will work in your favor. Things may seem to naturally fall into place when you are focused on the now. One event will happen that will lead to another and so on. It's a positive domino effect!

On the other hand, when you are thinking, worrying, and fretting about past events, beliefs or situations, synchronicity won't work in your favor. These thoughts are zapping your natural power and you don't have as much energy to allow synchronicity to be on your side.

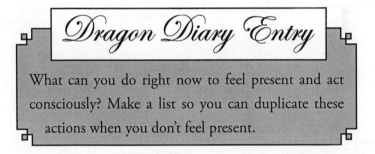

Dragon Diary Entry

What can you do right now to feel present and act consciously? Make a list so you can duplicate these actions when you don't feel present.

Environments

"Katie," is a medical intuitive and clairvoyant. She sees the emotional baggage that we hold in our bodies in the form of disrupted energy. There is one area in the body that she describes that looks like a planter with flowers. Depending on the person, seeds may be planted, sometimes they have grown and other times they may be straying or wilted weeds. If a seed is planted in a nourishing and nurturing environment, the seed can't help but grow to its full potential because more energy is provided for its growth.

What would you be like if you were born in a different place? Who would you have been then? Would you BE the same person? Your beliefs, habits, and behaviors may be very different. Wouldn't they? As the saying goes, you are a product of your environment.

Dragon Diary Entry

Are you placing yourself in a nurturing environment for your mind, body, and soul to express its utmost beauty and potential? What can you do to create a better environment? Where you can flourish? Are you in a nurturing environment? Why do you believe this to be the case? What can you do right now to change it?

Friends, Family & Lovers

> "Stay with friends who support you in these. Talk with them about sacred texts, and how you are doing, and how they are doing, and keep your practices together."
> ~ Rumi

Let's start with your first lessons. Ones you received from your family! What beliefs and perceptions have been fed to you without you consciously choosing to accept those beliefs? How have you been conditioned? What do you believe and why do you believe it? Your first beliefs came from your parents. You developed deeper beliefs from school peers and girlfriends/boyfriends relationships. Growing up, what would your friends say if you said, "I am going to be President." They would probably laugh in disbelief. Have you picked up on their disbelief? When did you step up and choose your own beliefs? Maybe you have -- good for you! Start today by surrounding yourself with people and influences who support your purpose and dreams. And know how special you are. This is your life after all!

> **"Opinions are the cheapest commodities on earth."**
> **~Napoleon Hill, Think and Grow Rich.**

Do you trust yourself? When you have a decision to make do you stop and ask your top five friends what they would do? Why would they know the answer and you wouldn't? Why wouldn't you trust yourself? I am not saying that you shouldn't share and talk through your ideas with others, but notice when you have been persuaded by their opinions. The habit of trusting yourself is definitely a process in training the mind. I challenge you to try it.

I wouldn't go so far as to say you shouldn't seek advice, but seek it from someone who has had success with a similar situation.

I had a client come to me after a few years of struggling to grow her business. I asked her how she was currently marketing her business. She said that she was going to network groups and taking their advice. A big alarm went off in my head. She was asking for marketing advice from others that were struggling. If you need advice, seek advice from successful people and organizations.

Dragon Diary Entry

Take a moment and think about some of your past decisions. Have you asked for opinions from others? Why have you asked for input? Was it to gather experimental information or was it that you didn't trust your own opinion? How did you use the information you received?

Can you let go of the opinions and beliefs from your family and friends? Can you awaken and empower your inner soul? Can you be the individual you were born to be? You can choose consciously what you believe. You can choose what you want your life to be like. You decide. Your past relationships may be hurtful. Move away from what they believe. You can now choose if you want to be hurt. YOU choose.

DRAGON MASTERS
Choose nurturing relationships.

On some level you can separate yourself from harmful relationships. If you are depressed, you will attract other depressed people. If you are an angry person, you naturally attract angry people. If you are happy, you attract happy people. Everyone mirrors you. Look at your friends and other relationships and observe themes in your relationships. For example, if all your friends are positive and energetic, you probably are positive and energetic. In my business, I have found that I naturally attract entrepreneurs who are ready to take a no-excuses approach to their business/marketing and mindset. I attract entrepreneurs with my similar characteristics. The people you attract mirror you. If you don't like what you see in your friends, you might want to consider changing your attitudes and thoughts. If you hang out with complainers, gossipers, judgers and other negative people you probably are one. The universal law of attraction states, "like energies attract like energies." This may mean you are a complainer, gossiper, judger, or a negative person, or that your energies are aligned with these energies.

"Sarah," a financial advisor, had left one bad relationship after another. She lived with a constant feeling of loneliness and depression. She contacted me when she just couldn't seem to build up her clientele as fast as her associates.

Sarah was losing her natural energy and power to choose her feelings. My immediate advice for Sarah was for her to empower herself. I offered her practices to explore self-love, self-esteem and confidence. Within three weeks, Sarah began to get clients on a more regular basis and attracted a boyfriend a couple of weeks later.

Make big boundaries! People respect people with defined personal boundaries. If someone is saying or doing something that bothers you, don't hold it in. Let it go by putting your boundaries into action.

I like to set boundaries with these four steps.

Inform: Inform the person what bothered you

without anger. Start with "I want you to know that..." They may not even be aware of what they did.

Request: "I request that ... "

Demand: "I insist that you ... " You can add consequences. "I insist that you stop or I will no longer coach you."

Leave: Stop associating with them. Leave the room. Put the child in time out. Leave either temporarily or permanently.

Dragon Diary Entry

Are you choosing relationships that nurture and support your growth? List all relationships that may be hindering your growth. What can you do right now to change it?

Vital Energy

Is your biography your biology? Yes. Look at it like this. If you drink too much caffeine and it causes you to feel anxious, your body responds physically to the caffeine. If through life experience you feel anxious, your body physically holds that as well. Physical tissues respond to stress from the inside and outside. Overeating and excessive food behaviors cause stress in the body. You hear this often when you have high blood pressure and the doctor tells you to reduce stress and eat better. Eating poorly zaps your energy just as much as the emotion of depression. They both steal valuable vital energy from you.

> **"The body's inability to metabolize foods that are not fresh results in the formation of ama, or toxic undigested material"**
> **Shubhra Krishan**
> *Essential Ayurveda: What It Is and What It Can Do for You*

From an Ayurvedic nutrition standpoint, processed foods or foods that are no longer fresh (overly cooked and processed foods) can disrupt prana or chi. *Ama* (or toxins in the body) clogs the natural energy channels in your body. These channels can be physical (ie arteries) or they can be nonphysical energetic channels called *nadis* (river or stream) through which your energy flows. *Ama* toxicity accumulates where there is a weakness in the body, and this will result in disease or dis-ease (mind indigestion, coated tongue, tight muscles).

Most parents have been brought up as children to believe that food gives us energy and replenishes the body no matter what the food. However, if food lacks vital energy, then you lack the nutrients for optimal health on a physical and emotional level.

Is this the same energy that connects you to your spirit? I believe clear channel energy comes from a healthy conscious being. What do you believe?

Dragon Diary Entry

How is your daily food intake helping you honor your body? Can you become more conscious about what you are putting in your body? What changes do you want to make? What are you willing to change now? What are you willing to change in the future?

Rule #4:
Be Inspired

> *"Every person who wins in any undertaking must be willing to burn his ships and cut all sources of retreat. Only by so doing can one be sure of maintaining that state of mind known as a BURNING DESIRE TO WIN, essential to success"*
> ~ Napoleon Hill

UNKINK YOUR MIND and allow inspiration in. Let's start with the secret to my success. I follow "The Inspiration Formula" or IDDA:

1. Inspiration causes desire
2. Desire causes determination
3. Determination causes action
4. Action causes creation

You feel emotions differently depending on your past wounds. For example, if you received straight A's all through school and everyone told you how smart you were, then when you became an adult, someone told you that you are stupid you may think they were out of their mind; you can't believe it is true. However, if your grades were sub par, you may feel upset when someone tells you that you are stupid. You take it to heart because you believe it to be true. We don't all feel the same way because we all have different past experiences, which mean different dragons.

No one can "make" you feel a certain way. You choose every one of your feelings. The associated feelings depend on the individual and the dragons or past behavioral patterns that have been created in their mind. Even if you are in a pattern of reacting and responding and you haven't learned a healthy way to let go and feel complete, you can choose to suppress or express your emotions. Suppression is holding your emotions in. When these emotions are held in, you begin to hide and cover your true authentic self. You stop listening to your inner truth.

> *When genuine passion moves you, say what you've got to say, and say it hot.*
> ~ D. H. Lawrence

DRAGON MASTERS
Express their emotions.

Make an intention to express and no longer suppress your emotions. This will open you up to a world of love, joy and abundance.

Your emotions are associated with your past emotional wounds. There are emotions that come up when you are "in the moment." For example, feeling sad during a movie or feeling happy after you win a soccer game. These are "in the moment" healthy expressions that allow you to express instead of suppress. You experience and feel your emotions fully. Feelings of disappointment or anger are great emotions to feel "in the moment." When these emotions come up, choose to feel them and then let them go for good.

Every emotion you have causes a physical response. You feel your emotions in your body. Right? Where else could you feel them? You also hold past emotional responses in your body. If you were bitten by a big dog as a child (knowledge is hidden in the mind) your body may emotionally react (subconscious mind) when you see a big dog in the present moment. This is a fear that has been suppressed. This is a dragon.

Dragon Diary Entry

Do I express my emotions as I feel them? What have I suppressed? Am I holding on to this wound for a reason? Is there some benefit to holding on to this wound? How can I let go of these suppressed emotions? Do I need to tell others they have hurt me? Do I need to write it down and burn the paper as I let go of the suppressed feelings? What will free me?

Emotional Dragon = present event + conscious thought + feeling based on past experience.

Example 1:
Fear dragon = you see big dog (in the present moment) + you think about past bite + you feel afraid.

Others may have grown up with a big, loving dog as a child and aren't bothered when they see a big dog. In fact, it might activate a pleasant memory.

Emotional Toxins

Let me ask you ... the fear (seeing big dog) dragon where

is it when you aren't seeing the dog or emotionally feeling the fear? Not only is it in your subconscious mind, it's also hidden in the physical fabric of the body. The emotions that you don't let go through expression create energetic holds in the body. Emotional suppressions literally block your natural energetic flow, affect your immune system and make you sick. You know this already by the recommendations to lower stress levels for your health.

When you continually suppress emotions, you begin to hold a source of your energy in the past. These emotions are also holding you in your emotional past. It is excess baggage that is keeping you from moving with ease and flow down your divine path.

> ❝You take the blue pill - the story ends, you wake up in your bed and believe whatever you want to believe. You take the red pill - you stay in Wonderland and I show you how deep the rabbit-hole goes.❞
> ~ Morpheus from The Matrix movie

You have a choice:

    A) The Red Pill that contains:
        Unconscious Thoughts + Reactive Emotions +

Reactive Action = Previous Results.

B) The Blue Pill contains:

Deliberate Thoughts + Deliberate Emotions + Deliberate Action = Fast and Deliberate Creation

Did you choose the Blue? Shall we continue?

Need-Driven Desires vs. Inspiration

"...all pain and suffering arises solely from the ego and not from God."
~ David Hawkins

Our mind is full of both "insipid" and "inspired" thoughts. As you learn the difference between need-driven desires and inspiration, please notice and observe how you feel when you have a need-driven desire versus an inspired desire. Which ones are from past programming and which are spirit-driven? You will find more thoughts are inspired than you ever thought possible. Let's explore our desires.

Need-Driven Desires

Need-driven desires are typically inner desires to have something in an attempt to fulfill an unmet need. An example of these desires may be a car or shoes you desperately want. You think you just want shoes, right? However, the shoes you desire might offer external recognition and validation because you are in need of recognition. I am not saying you should never desire material possession. I am suggesting you know <u>why</u> you have these desires.

When a situation is in question, ask yourself and be truthful with yourself. Do I want this <u>(thing)</u> to fulfill a need of security, social-acceptance, or self-acceptance?

Dragon Diary Entry

Look for areas in your life where something you dislike or struggle with continues to happen. Ask yourself and be truthful with yourself. Do I want this <u>(thing)</u> or make this <u>(thing)</u> happen to fulfill my need for security, social-acceptance, or self-acceptance? If this is the case, please Write it in your journal for possible mental (dragon) retraining and mastering.

You may feel in some way incomplete, unworthy or not good enough. The truth is, you aren't incomplete. You were born a genius. Life events, stories and situations birthed and grew mental patterns and now you are living with some wild dragons in your mind. We will start training these dragons soon enough, but for now please take the time to fully understand these basic concepts about how your mind works.

Our contemporary culture has duped us to feel as if we deserve stuff. It seems like we are all out to get more, have more and be more. Many people feel they are entitled to having all their needs and desires fulfilled. Period.

The universe is about GIVING, NOT GETTING. By fulfilling your inner emotional needs, you are available to give love, self-confidence and security in abundance. This mean you give love, respect and talent to others. This also means you give God-given services and sometimes it is in exchange for money. Just because someone pays you doesn't mean you are not giving.

When you overflow with gratitude and fulfillment, you attract others that are the same. Stop trying to GET something. I hear it all the time, "I seek recognition or I'm not confident enough." Have you ever heard the phrase: "What you focus on expands?" If you stop focusing on the lack or wanting and start focusing on empowering and willing yourself to be complete -- your world will shift! When you have self-respect you attract others with self-respect and they respect you. Like I said in the last chapter, you resonate with others who are similar to you. The truth is, if you interact with people that have bad habits, you may want to look at yourself. Others mirror you. They can't help but mirror you. We attract the energies with which we are in alignment. This satisfies the universal principle of like energies attract like energies.

Your spirit is powerful. Instead of seeking needs, start to feel present, alive, complete and already nourished internally.

Dragon Diary Entry

Write down everything you do in daily life that makes you feel love for yourself. This may include meditation, massage, or family time. Next to each item include WHY you think those things make you feel this way. For example, massage may offer love, comfort and self-acceptance. How can you allow the universe to guide you to what you need? What needs are you trying to fulfill when you find yourself with attachments (ie. stylish clothes, fast cars)?

> *There are two processes necessary for self-actualization: self exploration and action. The deeper the self exploration, the closer one comes to self-actualization.*
> ~ Abraham Maslow

Let's take a brief look at Maslow's Hierarchy of Needs to learn what needs you may be seeking to fulfill. Maslow's Hierarchy addresses our human needs and the underlying reason why we may do the things we do. The model builds on each level. It starts with our physiological needs then continues with our needs for feeling secure, social acceptance and love, and self-acceptance. The top section represents divine presence and enlightenment or what Maslow calls self-actualization.

Inspiration

Inspiration is simply dreams, fantasies, feelings, and heart-felt insights that reside in your mind and are available to you through spirit. Without inspiration there would be no creation.

Inspired: Of such surpassing brilliance or excellence as to suggest divine inspiration. ~ Webster's New Collegiate Dictionary

Some people can identify inspired thoughts while others can't. Oftentimes, inspiration strikes you suddenly, without warning, you may think, "I have no idea where that came from." You may call it an "epiphany." One word of caution: Inspired thoughts occur everyday and sometimes all day. Please pay attention to your inspired thoughts and take fearless action towards accomplishing the ones you choose.

How do you know what thoughts are inspired and what thoughts are coming from your previously created perceptions and beliefs? Test yourself! If you feel excited, energized, and terrific about the thought, it is inspired. You can also ask your inner guidance system by just asking yourself this question: Why not ask, "Is this thought, idea or feeling based on my past taught beliefs or is this inspired?" A "yes" or "no" usually comes back quickly. Go with what comes back right away. If nothing comes back, let it go for now and ask later.

> **"...the inspiration comes from the unconscious."**
> **Joseph Campbell, The Power of Myth**

In fact, inspiration is communicated to us from the collective unconscious mind in the form of vibration. It manifests itself in a way that really isn't language, but a feeling or vibration. When you experience this feeling of inspiration it may challenges your belief systems. In fact it may challenge your beliefs so much that you discard it completely. Your dragon-like mind gobbles up your inspiration without further thought or consideration.

Inspired thoughts are thoughts from the universal mind and inspired by God. Whatever you desire, you can accomplish. You receive divine/inspired desires with your God-given talents. One reason we don't all have the same desires is because we are unique individuals with unique talents. The only limits to what you can attain are the limiting belief patterns or dragons you have programmed in your mind. The truth of the matter is you wouldn't be inspired by things you could not make a reality. You are designed with unique desires so you can create a life by your design. If you believe it, you can achieve it.

The history of the light bulb offers a good example of collective unconsciousness and universal awareness. The history goes back much further than Thomas Edison. In Ancient Egypt is a temple called "Dendera" where wall art indicates that these Ancient Egyptians might have had some source of light. What has been seen is a form of a bulb, with a snake-like creature inside it. At the small end of the bulb is a cord-like connection that looks like a lotus flower with a long stem connected to a source box. The wall art looks very much like a bulb connected with a cord to an electric box. The knowledge to create an electric light bulb was already available to us. Thomas Edison didn't create the light bulb. In fact, he took a 50 year-old idea and improved it with a longer lasting source of light. He was inspired to do so. Also, as you may know, he didn't get it on the first try. He had to make countless mistakes. Just because something is inspired doesn't mean that it is the perfect solution. You have to fearlessly allow yourself to experience the journey.

DRAGON MASTERS

**Know mistakes are an important part
of the journey to success.**

When you can tap into a clear, open universal mind, feel inspiration and take fearless actions, you become unstoppable! The question then becomes how far do you WANT to go, not how far CAN you go.

Dragon Diary Entry

When was the last time you felt inspired? What can you do to feel inspired more often?

Divine Talents

"Take the talent from him and give it to the one who has the ten talents. 29For everyone who has will be given more, and he will have an abundance. Whoever does not have, even what he has will be taken from him."
~Parable of Talents, Matthew 25:28-29

The parable demonstrates the universal principle of the law of attraction, but also takes it a step deeper. My interpretation is, those who use their innate talents will live abundant lives. Those that run in fear and hide their God-given talents are negligent of God's will. When your talent is hidden behind limiting beliefs such as fear, you don't put your divine ideas into action and live abundantly. Your divine inheritance is ideas, not a bag of stuff or gold. It's your job to put your ideas to work to create a life of abundance.

Dragon Diary Entry

What are my talents? How can I use my talents everyday? Please note: These may or may not be talents used to make income.

Rule #5:
Empower Yourself

> **"You are choosing your creations as you are choosing your thoughts."**
> *~ Abraham-Hicks*

WHAT'S YOUR EXCUSE? Are you operating at your highest potential? No? Why do you think that is? Is some other event, resource or person getting in your way? Is something outside of you holding you back? Is it lack of time? Maybe it's education, money or health? These thoughts of lack could go on and on. Could it possibly be that you have something inside you that is dying to express your potential, but you are afraid to let it out? Often times instead of facing the reality and being 100% responsible for our lives, we hide from ourselves and blame others. We begin to only focus on our weaknesses and not our strengths.

DRAGON MASTERS

Take 100% responsibility and credit for every thought, image, mental pattern and emotion (T.I.M.E.) they experience.

The universe always has your best interest in mind. Why would there be reason to doubt or fear thoughts, images and emotions that are divinely inspired? You can have 100% faith to move forward with your passions and dreams.

> *"Faith and fear cannot occupy the same space"*
> *~Dick Gregory*

If you think reading this isn't a sign that you are ready to let go of the past and empower your present moment, you are mistaken. Now is the time to empower yourself. The universe sprinkles desirable ideas in to your mind/dungeon. Are you going to jump out of your hiding place and make them happen?

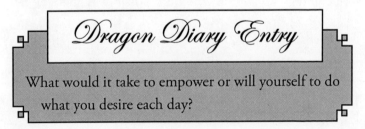

Dragon Diary Entry

What would it take to empower or will yourself to do what you desire each day?

Choice

Choices are opportunities or obstacles that cause you to make a decision. Many people make unconscious choices all day long by responding to their emotions and perceptions. They are completely unaware they are weighing their options and making choices based on their current perceptions.

The small area between choices and decisions has always been a fuzzy one for me. I often attract too many choices that are all desirable. With so many opportunities it is often hard to make a decision.

Dragon Diary Entry

When you have numerous choices, what variables do you weigh to make confident decisions? They may include your values -- time, energy, money etc. Write these variables down. Next time you have to make a difficult decision, use these variables to help you make a decision with ease.

There are two types of people that perceive choices very differently.

I'm Going to DO IT!

"Feeling Good"

Take FEARLESS action

Type 1:

- They listen to inspirations and divine thought, image and emotional vibrations.
- They focus and choose to manifest divine inspirations.
- They feel as if they have already accomplished the inspiration.
- They change their subconscious mind with regular images and visions.
- They take fearless action.
- They receive their desire.

Type 2:

- They observe their present results.
- They focus on what they don't have.
- They feel their present experience, and even worse, they may feel doubt, despair, and fear.
- They don't change their subconscious mind with their thoughts, images and visions.
- They take the same action they have always taken.
- They receive their present results.

If problems continue to persist in your life, and you continue to stay caught up in the struggle then you are in alignment with your problems. You will continue to attract these same types of problems into your life until you change yourself internally. The change must occur in your perceptions i.e. how you see and feel things in your mind and body. When you focus on the positive creations, you begin to naturally bring those creations into your life.

When we were searching for our next home, I told someone that I wanted a pool for the kids. He tried to talk me out of having a pool. He told me about the difficult upkeep and the danger of our youngest child drowning. I found myself using mental capacity by thinking, "I don't need to burden myself with this person's *worrying* opinion. I need to live presently, experience life and focus on what I desire." And that's when I realized I had fully empowered myself to choose my thoughts, images and emotions.

Experience with Imagination

Life is not about things, it's about the experience those things give you
~ Jen Blackert

Do you have a clear picture of your future? This is where you can use those visualization techniques you have probably already begun to explore. Here are a few visualization techniques I suggest.

Experience 1: The Sensory – Feel as if

Start 'The Sensory' experience by engaging all the senses, both internally and externally. What do you hear, see, feel, smell and taste?

Please note that 'The Sensory' is about what you experience, not what you see in your mind. You may discover that you don't actually need a new car, you just want to feel the experience of having a car that only wealthy people own.

Example: If you want a new car. Ask yourself…
   - What do I *hear* (while in the car of your dreams)? A quiet, sounding engine hum?
   - What do I *see* (while in the car of your dreams)? A brand new steering wheel with a top of the line sound system at my fingertips?
   - What do I *smell* (while in the car of your dreams)? Mmmm, that new car smell?
   - What do I *feel* (while in the car of your dreams)? The steering wheel feels smooth under my hands?

- What do I *taste* (while in the car of your dreams)? The new car smell tastes sweet?

A note of precaution: Feeling as if or acting as if does not mean you go out and start buying the things you can't afford. It means you begin to feel grateful for the things in your life. Feel as if you already have what you desire, this causes the universe to shift and opportunities will present themselves.

Experience 2: The Virtual

Engage in a virtual reality. Use your imagination in vivid detail.

Example: Visualize and feel what it is like to own, drive and experience the car of your dreams. It might help if you physically went to the dealership and test-drove the car. Visualize your interaction with the sales person while you are purchasing the car. How do you feel when you own this car? How can you feel this way now? Can you imagine that you are in your dream vehicle while in your current vehicle?

Experience 3: The Movie

See yourself as a curious observer as you view yourself participating in your dream. Can you see yourself watching a movie or seeing a play in which you are the star. Watch yourself act out the entire role.

Example: Relax, take some deep breaths and close your eyes and start watching yourself as if you are in the movie. The movie ends with you driving your new car into your driveway.

Experience 4: The Finish Line

Encode the experience in your being by seeing yourself achieving the goal and feeling the gifts of achieving the goal. What emotions can you attach to the outcome?

Example: How do you know when you have accomplished the goal or desire? Are you writing a final payment check? Are you driving your new car home? Are you enjoying the radio system in your new car? How will you know you accomplished your desire?

Experience 5: External Pictures with Internal Focus

Collect pictures of ideas, concepts and things you desire. Imagine yourself or put a picture of yourself in these pictures.

Example: A picture of you in your new car could be posted on your bathroom mirror. Be creative. Think about how you can remind yourself to see your future vision daily.

Practice your chosen visualization daily. Schedule it on your calendar for five minutes a day. Activate your imagination! Failure is not an option! What does your vision look like? Accept this idea or concept as the truth.

Throughout the day (everyday), keep your head clear and listen for the next piece (inspired thought or action) in your vision puzzle. Your vision is coming to you as long as you take the next inspired action fearlessly and live resistant free.

Visualization Experience Warning: Watch out for "Head-In-Clouds-Syndrome." Learn from John. "John," a small business owner, came to me because he was having trouble manifesting his vision. He said he had been seriously trying to reach his goals for six months. He told me he spent a lot of his time concentrating and focusing his thoughts on making more money. He was extremely unsatisfied with where his business was currently. He mentioned many times how unsatisfied he felt with his business.

The first change I asked John to make was for him to feel happy with his current success. John was spending mental energy on what he wanted in his future, but was passing up opportunities to achieve this success. He was offered advice that he ignored because, well ... he was not really sure why. I intuitively felt he was fearful that the advice would take time to implement and John didn't have confidence the effort would pay off.

Consider this. If your mind is in the clouds, you can't be present and consciously aware of what you are attracting. If you unconsciously ignore your attractions, how can you take the next appropriate action to manifest your future dream? This does not mean you should not consciously visualize or plan for the future. Instead choose to take present moments to visualize your future desires. This is something you can schedule into your day. Don't let your future visions become another cluttering thought in your mind.

Example: You are taking a bath and choose consciously to visualize about your future dream home. You experience your new home in your mind. When you step out from a delicious bath, you choose to be present by feeling the cool air on your wet skin and you notice the fluffy towel's texture on your back. You experience the present moment. You choose to feel vs. think. And maybe you can feel as if you are already in your new home. Don't just think about it. Create images and feel as if your vision is already a part of your reality and it soon will be.

Please note. It's important to understand what you desire is already available -- it's in the non-physical form. You are changing yourself internally as you visualize and experience a different future. Continue to use regular visualization to burn this image into your subconscious mind. When an image is burned on to the subconscious mind, you can't help but create the physical manifestation of it.

Mantras

Mantras are words or phrases repeated over and over to help achieve this relaxed state of mind and burn images on your subconscious mind.

Ancient religions believed mantras had mystical powers. Maybe that's because they are very effective at engraining messages in our subconscious minds.

"Tess," a self proclaimed "workaholic," filled every minute of every day with work and family activities. She rushed here and there and everywhere. She continually complained about not having enough time.

Tess was in a repeated pattern of always filling her days with activities. My coaching advice to Tess was to sit quietly for 10 minutes each day and create some space in her mind with the mantra, "I always have plenty of time." Free time and the image of free time will create more free time. Before long, she had a couple of evenings free each week. Tess was sending an energetic vibration out to the universe to "not have enough time." This meant she was attracting more of the same—"not have enough time." You see how this works? The universe obediently agreed and gave Tess exactly what she requested. Tess learned to express her feelings differently. She started a mantra that said, "I always have more time than I need and I am very grateful." Tess soon had more free time to enjoy herself.

Dragon Diary Entry

Take a moment to write down any mantras you may want to implement into your life. They go something like this... "I choose to be a strong woman that always gets exactly what I desire," or, "I always have more money than I need." When you repeat the mantra see if you can see a visual picture that matches.

Choosing Emotions

Amp up your rate of creation with unwavering emotions and feelings associated with your visions and mantras. Connect your unmanifested vision/mantra with emotions of gratitude, delight, love, and excitement.

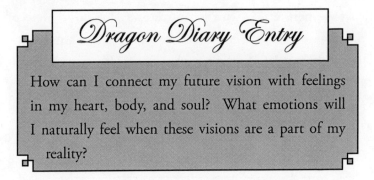

Dragon Diary Entry

How can I connect my future vision with feelings in my heart, body, and soul? What emotions will I naturally feel when these visions are a part of my reality?

Emotional Freedom

Emotional freedom occurs when you choose your emotional responses and you no longer feel like an emotionally victim to circumstances. You learn to accept your emotions as you accept the truth. You don't fight or resist your emotions. You learn to listen to your inner intelligence. Emotional freedom helps you align your whole being with your feelings.

Are you having trouble dealing with these unwavering

emotions associated with your vision? Maybe you are having trouble controlling your negative emotions in daily life. Or maybe you feel your emotions of fear, doubt, and discontentment are stopping you from living the life of your dreams. If these scenarios sound familiar, you may want to consider changing your emotional responses with proven techniques. Some examples include:

- NLP (Neuro-Linguistic Programming) NLP is similar to hypnosis but uses techniques that can be used in daily life to remind yourself to change your beliefs.
- EFT (Emotional Freedom Technique) This technique addresses the belief and releases it from your subconscious hard drive.
- EDF (Emotional Dragon Freedom Method) This method is my own creation based on the two techniques above. It works as follows:

Emotional Dragon Freedom Method

When we take ourselves out of life's whirlwind, and in that moment focus on our inner being, we can see the truth, and the crippling negative emotion fades. Oftentimes, emotions of doubt, fear, and discontentment are false perceptions.

My Emotional Dragon Freedom Method (EDF) brings about an emotional shift. It doesn't always take the emotion away, but this method quickly lessens the degree of the emotional intensity. For example, if you rate your emotional fear as a 10, you may find that after you practice the Emotional Dragon Freedom Method, your emotional fear may drop to 7.

Here's how to practice 'The Emotional Dragon Freedom Method':

Rate the emotional feeling you want freedom from on a scale from 1-10. It could be fear, anxiety, depression, cravings, anger – you name it.

Step 1: Inhale and hold your breath. Meanwhile state the phrase: I feel (*put feeling here*), but I completely accept this feeling as I accept myself. (Holding the breath naturally relaxes the nervous system and that is why it is an important part of this method.)

Step 2: While holding your breath, state the change: I know that this is just a feeling and I choose to be (*put replacement feeling here.*) I choose to be (*put replacement feeling here.*) I choose to be (*put replacement feeling here*.) I choose to be (*put replacement feeling here*.) I choose to be (*put replacement feeling here*.)

Step 3: Rinse and repeat. I usually tell clients to go through the whole cycle approximately 10 times.

Let's look at what I call "Oscar -- the overwhelmed obsessive dragon" as an example:

Rate the overwhelm feeling. Inhale and hold the breath. Say clearly to yourself, "Although I feel *overwhelmed*, I completely accept this feeling as I accept myself. I know that this is just a feeling and I choose to be *calm and peaceful.* I choose to be *calm and peaceful.* I choose to be *calm and peaceful*. I choose to be *calm and peaceful.* I choose to be *calm and peaceful.*"

Exhale and rate the feeling again. Repeat the cycle up to 10.

Rule #6:
Know Your Dragons

> "The definition of insanity is
> doing the same thing over and over and
> expecting different results."
> ~ Benjamin Franklin

THERE'S A SMALL SQUIRREL IN MY BACKYARD
running with an acorn. I watch him for a minute when
suddenly he is attacked by another squirrel attempting to
steal his acorn. After a long struggle the smaller squirrel
runs away, unfortunately without his acorn. I wonder if
that squirrel will still be holding angry thoughts toward the
squirrel that sold his dinner?

No other life form on planet Earth seems to hold so much

negativity in their mind, body, and life as the human race. Think about it, you may see an angry squirrel chasing another for an acorn, but I bet the anger is forgotten once the other squirrel has eaten the acorn. Wouldn't you agree?

There are millions of patterns in the mind. The patterns that actually work for you can be left alone, but the patterns

that aren't working can be explored and retrained. In addition to our own individual dragon patterns, I've discovered seven king dragon patterns that exist in the minds of many people. These dragons are stopping you from living the life of your dreams.

Seven King Dragons

In this section, I discuss the seven king dragons and in the next section I discuss how you can uncover your own unique hidden limiting beliefs and mental patterns (dragons).

Note: These seven dragons a.k.a. limiting beliefs are not personality types such as found in Myers-Briggs or DISK, but limiting beliefs and behaviors. Are you ready to remove the limits in your mind? Let's meet the seven king dragons in our mind!

Careful. There's a dragon on the next page.

King Dragon #1:

Mental Incongruent "Mindy" Dragon

"Mindy", the mental incongruent dragoon, has a mind of a two-year old. When your habits and behaviors are not in alignment with your inspirations, aspirations and goals, Mindy is usually the reason. She is in your mind stomping her feet and causing tantrums and chaos. Mindy doesn't want you to make changes. She feels safe right where she is.

Do you carry on a conversation with yourself? Maybe you are questioning yourself and your thoughts? Do you tell yourself about all the things that you "should" be doing, but never take the action to make it happen?

Here's the key point! When you find yourself talking negatively to yourself ... BOOM! Say hi to Mindy. This is different than deliberately talking to yourself. Examples include carrying on a conversation with yourself that is in conflict with your unconscious habits. Other examples include calling yourself "stupid, unworthy, or ugly." Or maybe you hear conflicting thoughts like these.

"I want to lose weight" and "I want ice cream"
"I want another bottle of soda"
"Wow. I can't believe that was $120. Maybe I *should* return it."

"I *shouldn't* have another cup of coffee"

"I want that dress" and "That's too much to spend"

Mindy is around when you have the desire to eat, but you are not hungry. (Mindy is telling you to eat). It's annoying, isn't it? The dragon is the subconscious behavior of eating when some event has happened. This event could be as simple as boredom. That thought in your head, "I want to eat, I just want to eat." Ah, that's the dragon. It's like a two-year old child demanding to be fed. RIGHT NOW! The dragon lives in the unconscious and subconscious dungeons of the mind.

To give a visual to Mindy... you may see her bounce back and forth to each thought across a line. The line divides the conscious and the unconscious minds.

This dragon-like behavior is fighting with the your conscious logical mind, which says, "I want to lose weight and I'm not hungry. Why would I eat?" Yet, something inside you says, "I want to eat." Which thought is the truth? Which thought can bring you what you want? Technically, they are both something you want. But when logical thought is congruent with unconscious habits and behaviors, you feel more complete and congruent.

The first step to obtaining a higher power of consciousness is to learn how to get your mind congruent with your unconscious and subconscious habits.

There are two reasons thoughts become incongruent.

1. Our desires aren't in alignment with our daily habits and behaviors.

For example: If you want to be rich, but you fill your time in other ways and avoid the projects that will make an impact -- you are out of alignment. It is time to make a change. Today. Misalignment of this type can come out in the form of procrastination, fear, or just plain lack of intention.

Someone once told me, "Self-discipline is self-respect." I pondered these words for weeks. I thought, "How can I nurture and honor my true being if I am forcing myself <u>not</u> to do something that it naturally desires." Suddenly, it was all very clear. If I wanted a different future, I had to change my past patterns and behaviors and tame the wild dragon. This dragon had been controlling my life. I was not consciously choosing! Finally, clarity!

2. Our thoughts aren't in integrity with our actions.

We are attracted to people who are authentic. There's so much in our world that's fake, false perception or a mere illusion, that it feels really good to be around someone who is full of integrity. The best way to get your mind in alignment with your desires is to be <u>in</u> integrity with yourself and everyone else.

What does it mean to be in integrity? It means to "seek truth." Never lie to yourself or anyone else. Don't forget to tell the truth to yourself about your money, body, and family! Never say you are going to start to exercise on Monday if you aren't. Never say you are going to start your diet if you aren't. Never tell yourself you are fat when you know you really aren't. If you are doing these things to yourself you need to stop. Cut it out! It causes chaos: mental chaos.

Do you believe you have integrity? If you tell yourself you are going to do something, do you always do it? Are there promises you are not keeping? Intentions you are not reaching? So many of us make promises but don't keep them. You might tell yourself, "I am going to start a diet on Monday." Monday comes and goes, and what happened? Did you lie to yourself? You did?! That means you are out of integrity with yourself.

You have to be in integrity with everyone, especially yourself. If you aren't in integrity with yourself, your mind stops believing you, then you are really in trouble. Remember, Mama always says, "Don't lie." When you start listening and living consciously, you can stay more aligned with what you really want and need. I believe, if you are not aligned with yourself, you cannot achieve your highest potential. If you say you are going to do something, you need to do it. Never lie to yourself or anyone else.

Dragon Diary Entry

List all the things in your life where you feel you may be out of alignment. Next to each item list a way to change. You may not feel you are able to change everything all at once so prioritize the ones you believe will make the biggest impact. Now, create a reminder system or plan of action to implement these new changes.

Helpful hint: Before you change any of your dragons, remember, that in order to change a dragon, you must give it awareness, attention, love, and focus because it has been neglected in the past.

Mental Congruence:

First, see the dragon in your mind's eye? What does she look like? Can you communicate with her? What would she say to you? What would it take to retrain her? Can you get her to change her attitude? Can you get her on board with your conscious logical thought?

Still stuck? Here are three questions you can share with Mindy.

1. Is this what I desire?
2. Is this aligned with my future path? This question reminds you to respect your future desires, by turning every "should" into a "could."
3. Is this for the greater good of myself and humankind?

This is not about willpower. These questions will completely change your subconscious mind over time. The key word here is ... over time! If you use these questions regularly, they will become a natural habit in your daily life. It may take some effort at first, but you can change your way of thinking completely and naturally attract what you want into your life.

Single Incongruent Thoughts:

Do you ever hear thoughts in your head that you wish you

didn't? Let me tell you... you CAN change your thoughts. For example when you hear the thought, "Why am I so frustrated?" Change the thought to the mirror opposite. When you hear the thought change it to say, "Wow, check out this challenge I get to solve." This tool has helped many clients that needed to overcome fear or gain self-confidence.

Don't skim over this! Changing your thoughts as you hear them can create a profound effect on your life. After time your dragon will naturally tell you what you want to hear. By changing these thoughts and believing something different, you can get rid of any limiting thoughts and change your life.

King Dragon #2:

Overwhelmed Obsessive "Oscar" Dragon

"Oscar", the overwhelmed and obsessive dragon, just can't let go of (past T.I.M.E.) thoughts, images, mental patterns and emotions of the past. Anytime you feel the feeling of overwhelmed or disruptive mental noise, an Oscar dragon is present. Oscar is the dragon that runs circles in your head and keeps you awake at night. These obsessive dragon-like thoughts could be about pending projects, past relationships, yesterday's food that you ate in abundance or just plain future worry.

An example of this dragon is if someone told you they didn't want to work with you because you were too demanding. Depending who you are, Oscar might drum up all kinds of thoughts. Then take each thought and run, run, run with it. Literally, run around in your head... up, down, and all around. You begin questioning every thing you do: pondering, questioning, and wondering what you could and should do next.

"Doris", a senior executive for a computer firm, was continually obsessing over her previous conversations with other associates. She has an obsessive fear that she should have said something differently or spoken more clearly. She suffered from low self-esteem and lack of confidence. She felt fearful her co-workers wouldn't like or trust her no matter what she did. I later learned this was because she was never trusted growing up. Her obsessive fears and thoughts were so consistent, she was actually attracting consequences to herself. When someone acts like they are untrustworthy, wouldn't you have reason to not trust them?

My advice for Doris was to visualize a dragon running circles in her mind. (One circle per thought to be exact.) This visualization and journaling allowed her to begin a dialog with Oscar. She would start with acknowledging and thanking the dragon for trying to protect her. Then she could kindly ask him to stop. Next, she could ask Oscar to replace the obsessive thoughts with a more truthful, positive thoughts. Lastly, she could anchor a thought to a physical action (like tapping her wrist) and deliberately repeat the action and new thought until it became a natural habit or the truth. When or if Oscar returned, she could continue to repeat these steps until the dragon behaved!

Helpful hint: When replacing these thoughts with more truthful, positive thoughts, be sure you feel good about the new thought. You are changing your belief system, so you have to feel it is (or could be) the truth for you.

Dragon Diary Entry

Review the last two or three times that your mind obsessed about something (good or bad)? Do you see any patterns? If work has been keeping you up at night, what action might detour Oscar's obsessive behavior?

Get Out of Overwhelm

Step 1: Visualize it him running in your head.

Step 2: Imagine each circle the dragon takes as a complete thought pattern. Write down what that thought pattern is. This may include a single thought, a feeling associated with that thought, then another escalating thought and another escalating feeling.

Step 3: Create a dialog (write it down) with Oscar. Ask him to change the thought. Or, see if he will let go of it completely when you tell him you have written down your next action step.

Step 4: Focus on the moment by taking about 30-50 deep breathes, count each breath and see if you can hold each one for 3-5 seconds. Rinse and repeat as needed.

King Dragon #3:

Decision Procrastination "Dino" Dragon

"Dino", the decision procrastination dragon, appears when you are faced to make a decision and you flee. Dino doesn't know what he wants. He's usually a multi-tasking master (or at least thinks he is). Dino is the master of creating chaos because he won't make a choice and go for it.

When you find you have a Dino dragon you need to find your footing. In other words, let go of the past and start over. Scrap all old "to do" lists and take a look at your life and business. Ask yourself, "What needs to happen next?"

Here a tip: If you can't decide what you want, how can the universe deliver it to you?

When "Cindy" came to me she wanted to explore Internet marketing for her coaching business. I emailed her to set up her first appointment and she responded that she was looking at other businesses – a business franchise. I told her that I would be here when she needed my help.

Then next time I heard from her she wanted to explore her coaching business again. Then she thought maybe she wanted to be a virtual assistant. Once we began working together, I found that this dragon was lurking in all areas of her life.

She had trouble shopping; she would buy something and

return it the next day. She would order something at a restaurant and complain when it arrived. Dino, the anti-decision dragon was active is many areas of her life.

Cindy and I worked together for six months to retrain this dragon. She learned how to feel more grounded and centered in her body. She also learned to make decisions without changing her mind later. She became more focused and decisive in all areas of her life.

"Sally" offers another example of Dino. Sally, an attorney, had a mental pattern that caused her to procrastinate on her decisions, especially one's that involved some kind of risk or a mistake. On some level she felt that her decision would jeopardize her security and self-esteem. Though these decisions were not actually risks to her security, they could have caused her to stretch her pocket book an inch or so beyond her comfort zone. When she fell out of her comfort zone, her pattern was to retreat and halt. She would postpone making a decision until the last minute, which sometimes caused the decision to be made for her. Until we talked on a deep level she actually considered herself a great decision maker.

I started to question her. We, first, explored the past to see if she knew where the procrastination came from. She shared with me that when she was six years old, her mom would take her to a fast food restaurant but would quickly leave and go somewhere else, saying she couldn't eat anything on the menu. Her mother was perceived as someone unable to make decisions. So, Sally was taught how to avoid making decisions. She learned as a child, if you procrastinate, a decision will be made for you.

The awareness of this pattern offered her mental space to exercise her power of choice. Now when a decision comes up, it offers her the opportunity to just decide, rather than wasting her valuable energy with turning it over and over in her mind.

Decision Making Process

Step 1: STOP!

Stop, breathe, start over. When we breathe - we inhale air and exhale air. Bring your attention to the space and silence between your inhalation and exhalation. In other words, hold your breath at the end of the inhalation, pause, and then exhale, pause and then inhale. Continue until you feel more conscious and focused.

Do this for 10-minutes. Reevaluate how present you feel afterwards.

Step 2: Check Your P.H. (Procrastination Habits)

I've discovered the root of indecision is procrastination. And, the root of procrastination is either the lack of motivation, confidence or fear. Finally, lack of inspiration comes from a lack of mental clarity/intuition, concentration, and focus on your true authentic and divine desires.

If you procrastinate, it is critical that you understand why you are procrastinating. This habit is guaranteed to slow down your rate of creation and success. What can you do if you find yourself procrastinating? The questions below will help you refocus and stop procrastinating.

> IMPLEMENTATION. Do I know how to implement the issue at hand?

> AVOIDANCE. Am I avoiding or ignoring it? Is it an unmet need (Security, Social Acceptance, Self Acceptance) that is causing me to procrastinate this decision?

> GATHERING INFORMATION. Am I searching for a solution or looking for information to help me make a decision?

Step 3: Make your decision with clarity and follow through.

Dragon Diary Entry

How often do you make solid decisions where you choose to do something and you do it — without hesitation? Do you always cut off all other possibilities once your decision is made? If not, what can you do to make better decisions with confidence?

King Dragon #4:

Attention-Deficit "Alice" Dragon

"Alice", the attention-deficit dragon, can't focus or concentrate on her desires long enough to accomplish them. She wants to DO more, BE more, HAVE more, yet she can't quiet the mental noise and allow things to come to her.

Get Focused

Take a moment to feel your body with your five senses internally. This doesn't have to take long.

Ask yourself: What are my lungs doing? My heart? Can I hear my heart? What does my inner body feel like? Scan your body.

Bring your focus to your senses. What do you feel, see, hear, taste, and smell both internally and externally? Do you see how you feel more conscious after this body-scan?

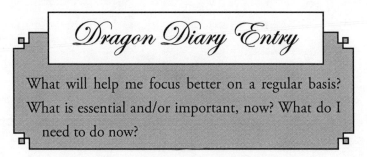

Dragon Diary Entry

What will help me focus better on a regular basis? What is essential and/or important, now? What do I need to do now?

Inner Discovery

If you have an Alice dragon in your mind, you may need to learn to look inside for answers. Never be ashamed about who you are. It is the inner truth you are seeking.

Step 1: Get quiet for a moment and realize that you are here now! You are reading while sitting on this couch or chair. You have nothing you need to do more than focus on what you are hearing and reading.

Step 2: Know the feelings of mental confusion and clutter are just feelings. You feel them inside yourself. No one feels the same feelings as you feel them. You are not your feelings -- you choose to feel them (so to speak). Find these feelings in your body and answer these questions. Where do these feelings exist? Will music, a movie or a fun evening out change these feelings? What do I need to feel differently. Once you identify the tightness in the body, breathe into these areas of your body.

Step 3: Question yourself:
- What is causing me to feel this way? (make a list)
- What can I do to change this feeling?
- What do I believe about this feeling?
- Why do I believe that?

- Is it the truth?
- What would make this the truth?
- What do I choose to believe?
- How do I choose to feel?
- What do you choose to believe? How do you choose to feel?

King Dragon #5:

Resistant "Ricky" Dragon

"Ricky", the resistant to change dragon, seems to struggle, avoid and resist anything that is out of his comfort zone.

> **"Opportunity often comes disguised in the form of misfortune, or temporary defeat"**
> **~Napoleon Hill**

What obstacles do you place in front of yourself? Are you making excuses for why you aren't successful? Are you resentful? Is it because you're afraid of risking your security? Is this an obstacle or an opportunity in disguise? What might you have to give up to take this opportunity (ie. time, money, travel)?

If you feel you are fleeing when approached with a challenge or an obstacle, yes, then you may need to take a good long look at your resistant Ricky dragon. You may believe it's a person, lack of time, or another type of obstacle. When you become aware of your obstacles, you can know when it is present. Whatever it is, I assure you that you put it there. You unconsciously placed this obstacle in front of you by your thought patterns and beliefs. You have millions of unconscious mental patterns that keep you operating in everyday life. Unfortunately, some of your unconscious patterns are not helping you to live the life of flow and ease that you desire. These unconscious patterns and beliefs are obeyed without any conscious thought.

But there is good news. Obstacles are often opportunities in disguise. Obstacles show up just outside of your own frame of reference. You see them as obstacles, but they may really be opportunities that the universe is offering you. It is your job to receive the universe's gifts.

> **"Opportunity is missed by most people because it is dressed in overalls and looks like work."**
> **-- Thomas Alva Edison**

Maybe you have attracted one of these opportunities into your life:

> You feel you have to take a risk, travel, work or spend money outside your comfort zone. You then respond with disappointment and maybe you begin to make excuses. You think, "Maybe I don't need this after all." Or, you start to justify with, "It may help me grow, but maybe there is another way. Maybe there's an easier or even cheaper way."

> Note: This is a pattern of response, could be risky. Remember, if you attract something into your life that you want and feel inspired to do

then you need to step up and fearlessly choose to accept it as a gift.

DRAGON MASTERS

Make decisions and take actions without hesitation or procrastination.

Zero Resistance

Remedy the Ricky dragon by learning the art of zero resistance! Zero resistance is about listening to your desires and taking action on your inspirations. Making swift decisions and taking immediate action is an art many people lack. I recommend taking immediate action before the feelings of fear, doubt, or anxiety creep in.

When an inspiring thought or action comes to you, the first questions should not be "How much" but "Do I want this in my life"? If the answer is, "Yes," then make your decision and then take immediate action. Just 'go' before the mad dragons enter into your head! In other words, take the appropriate action swiftly. Maybe you need to try a small experiment or qualifying test, but don't just discard what might be inspired destiny because of the cost.

Instead, think in terms of the value of the investment, not just an up-front price. Ask yourself, "What value does this bring to my life?" "What question does this answer for me?" "Is this the answer I have been trying to attract?" You will know when you have been inspired to take action. You will also know when you did not "seize the day."

Change your internal language by asking yourself...

1. Do I want this in my life?
2. What is the next action step I need to take to obtain this?
3. What do I need to do right now?

Success is about letting go, releasing, allowing, opening, and operating WITHOUT RESISTANCE! Too many people practicing these universal principles start visualizing but don't take action. They choose what they want, but they don't listen for inspiration and follow through with fearless action so they can manifest it.

Zero resistance does take practice and it will keep you moving toward your goals.

Resistant Areas

Do you feel that you are resisting change in your business or life? Here are four areas that I ask clients to seriously look at when I feel they are resisting change. I use the acronym T.H.E.M to remember.

1. Tools/Education/Skills
2. Habits/Behaviors
3. Environmental
4. Mindset/Perceptions

What comes up when you look at each area? Do you have all these components of success? What area needs improvement? Are you perceiving mental blocks that aren't true?

Dragon Diary Entry

What are your reasons for not making your dream come true? What challenges are you currently facing? Why are you facing these challenges? Make a list.

Are these reasons the truth? Or is it just a made up story? Can you stop believing these reasons? Do you need to get advice from others? What will create a shift?

King Dragon #6:

Money "Morgan" Dragon

"Morgan", the money challenged dragon, harbors fears about not having enough money. He worries and lacks the faith to allow money to flow in. His focus is often on the fear of failure instead of the desire for success because he wants to desperately force money to come to him.

To retrain this dragon, it's important to know what money is and how to attract it into your life.

Embrace the Money Rules:

1. Money is used. This means money never uses you. This includes the life sacrificing actions you take to receive it.

2. Money does not come to you by chance or luck. You choose to have an abundance of money.

3. Money matters when it's used. It should not be hoarded. It must circulate.

4. Money must flow like water. Is your money evaporating? Or is it accumulating? Where do you get in the way of your money's natural flow? Add a short journal entry.

If you fear and worry about money, money won't come to you. Remove those fears and have faith that money is coming to you in abundance. FEEL this abundance! I'll say that again. FEEL this abundance, now. Look for the things in life you naturally feel grateful for and focus your attention there. Stop focusing your attention on lack. When you are connected to your source of inspiration, you take the appropriate action required to position and align you with financial income.

5. Money is energy and comes to you through people not from people. Don't use people to receive money. Attract money energetically to you through people and stop chasing money. Whenever you chase something, it runs.

6. Money is not power! It's a tool.

Following The Financial Flow

Let's take a trip to the theatre. The first time you see a movie you are on the edge of your seat with anticipation. The second time you watch the same movie you feel more alert and present as you enjoy every moment. You know how it will end, there is no anticipation or anxiety about the end results -- this ALLOWS you to enjoy the unfolding story. Can your flow of money and life feel this same way?

Start a mantra: Repeat after me... "I am the master of my money." "Money flows in and out of my life as I choose and desire." "I am the master of my money." "I enjoy participating in the flow of my money." "I am the master of my money." "I love to observe my expenditures and the flow of my income."

Explore Your Bad Money Habits

Bad Habit #1: You don't tell the truth about money in your head.

You don't think you have enough or you spend what you don't have. Maybe you hide or avoid bills, delete messages or just avoid dealing with your finances. Get in the habit of telling the truth about your money. Are you spending money without thinking or looking at your debt? Are you using money as a tool or are you allowing your money to dictate your future expenditures?

Bad Habit #2: You don't plan how your money will be used.

Have you taken the time to create a financial forecast or plan? Or do you just drop money into a saving account and let it sit? Do you forecast what you will do with your future salary? How much you will earn or create?

Bad Habit #3: You neglect to focus on the big picture

Do you focus on your highest return on investment? Or do you let your day unfold without control? Do you carefully manage your time and delegate properly so you can spend your energies on your highest return investments?

Bad Habit #4: You hide your gifts and keep your divine talents a secret.

Choose to step up and take the necessary actions you need to make your life a thriving success. Some people hide because they lack confidence, security or love. What's your excuse?

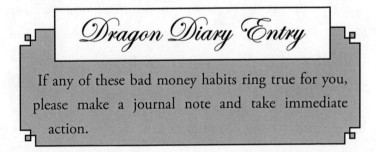

Dragon Diary Entry

If any of these bad money habits ring true for you, please make a journal note and take immediate action.

A Word About 'Thinking'

We think that we think, but what we really do is pull from

memory and experiences. Think about this for a moment. You know what you know so you pull from what you know. Ok, stay with me here. I am asking you to forget your reality for a minute. Forget what you know. What if you just landed here in this body at this moment and then I tell you that you are a multi-millionaire. You have no evidence. You don't check your bank account. You just operate as a millionaire. What would that feel like? Could you create this image in your head? Your subconscious mind can't tell the different between what is theory and fact. Can you feel this way all of the time?

The Money Mindset

We are surrounded by abundance. You see it everyday in nature. When I offer clients the steps to take to change their perception it always starts with our abundant world. The gift of what you have. Being grateful and consciously aware of your surrounding isn't always easy, but it is most definitely the place to start.

When you feel the feelings of lack, you are giving your energy to a perception. It's never the truth. The truth is the universe provides.

King Dragon #7:

Wanting-To-Be-Worthy "Wilma" Dragon

"Wilma", wanting-to-be-worthy dragon, usually has low self-esteem, a need for recognition from others, and just won't accept herself as she is. She doesn't feel important, fabulous or confident. Wilma seeks reasons to feel upset and affirm she isn't good enough. She looks for evidence and reasons that would prove she is worthy, but is so self-critical she finds very few. On some deep-seeded level, Wilma feels that if she is 'perfect' she might have a chance of measuring up to the rest of the world. Ironically, this dragon is never 'perfect' in her own eyes. Wilma thrives to be better than she thinks she is. She perceives that everything she does just isn't good enough. She believes that she must reach an intangible ideal or she's a complete failure. She doesn't understand that good may just be good enough.

Self-Esteem Builder

Step 1: Accept the dragon as a part of you and tell her that it is okay to view the world differently.

Step 2: Forgive all her past mistakes and leave them in the past so you can start fresh, without the baggage of not being perfect in the past. You were born perfect and whole!

Step 3: Teach your dragon how to set only realistic and flexible deadlines and goals. This will take presence and daily practice.

Step 4: Practice deadline completion and feel complete at the end of the project.

Step 5: Let go of judgments in all areas of your life. This includes judgment of yourself and others.

Step 6: Change your environment. Select friends, family, and other relations who accept you for who you are. Discard all others that you believe may be judging you.

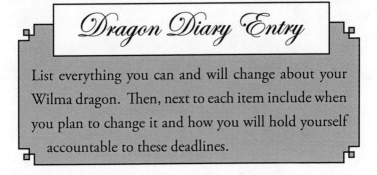

Dragon Diary Entry

List everything you can and will change about your Wilma dragon. Then, next to each item include when you plan to change it and how you will hold yourself accountable to these deadlines.

Your Unique Dragons

Observing the thoughts in your mind allow your thinking to be a choice instead of a mental record that repeats and skips in your mind. Wouldn't it be nice to live in a quiet spacious place and choose to use your brain when you would like? If you have several thoughts firing all at once, some peace and quiet is well deserved. Are you ready to choose what to think, feel, believe and create?

> *"Sow a thought, and you reap an act;*
> *Sow an act, and you reap a habit;*
> *Sow a habit, and you reap a character;*
> *Sow a character, and you reap a destiny."*
> *- Charles Reade*

You can let go of all the past ideas and beliefs that aren't serving you! You can believe something different. It doesn't matter what it is. Maybe your parents preached, "Money doesn't grow on trees." You took this information in and believed it without a second thought. You didn't consciously choose to believe it. What if it wasn't the truth? What if there was a money tree somewhere? If you think about it, oranges grow on trees. What if you had an orchard and sold the oranges? Would that be money growing on trees? Would that mean that money grows in abundance? What if you were born a child of Donald Trump? What would you believe then? Would you see things in a different light?

Are you ready to go on a dragon hunt ferreting out past beliefs that aren't serving you? Not memories, but beliefs that may be keeping you from the life you truly desire? You carry in your mind information and intellectual knowledge that has become an engrained belief, but it wasn't there when you were born. You created it.

Today if you are operating on beliefs and ideas from the past, then you will manifest yesterday's results. Tomorrow will bring the same result as yesterday and the day before and the day before. This pattern holds the mind in a vicious circle and you automatically continue manifesting yesterday's outcome. You must change internally to create something new.

DRAGON MASTERS
Notice and observe the present mind.

Contrary to popular Law of Attraction method, which tells us to give no attention to what we don't want, I believe awareness is the first step to unleashing your authentic self. By bringing awareness to your dragon-like patterns, you can begin to break the cycle. Awareness offers you an opportunity to break habits and behaviors.

Find YOUR Dragons: Defeating Dragon Discoveries

Read the list of common beliefs. If you can relate to one or more of them, jot down why you know for a fact that it is the TRUTH. Then ask, is it really the TRUTH? How can you experience this differently?

1. I have to work hard to make good money. What's your definition of 'hard?' Does it mean 'length of time', 'difficulty' or 'work your don't like?'

2. I can't charge a lot for what I do. I don't deserve it. Why do you believe you don't deserve to make more money?

3. I can't create this kind of wealth. I am not good enough. I don't have what it takes.

4. I am afraid of being thought of as a fake or a fraud.

5. I don't know how to _____. Remember your intuition will set you free. If you don't know how, maybe you just need to start asking. Asking others for help or for direction may be all you need.

If you can relate to any of these ideas, take the time to write them in your journal and get to the heart of the issue. The "Whying Method" (in the next chapter) helps you question your subconscious mind so you can uncover the truth to why you do the things you do.

Look at the facts! Get down to the truth! What is the story you are making up around this issue? Recreate a story that includes the truth.

Find YOUR Dragon: Feeling Stuck?

What blocks are you putting in your path to success? What is holding you back? Where are you stuck? What specifically are you giving your attention to? Is that where your attention should be?

When you feel stuck you may need to look for a dragon. This can be evidence of lack of knowledge, fear, or procrastination. It is important to figure out the source of the dragon. Where did this dragon come from? How can you let him go?

Get in the habit of noticing when you are stuck and ask yourself, "Why am I stuck?" "What can I do to get going again?" Often times you can quickly figure out what you may need to do next.

Find YOUR Dragons: Repeating Mistakes & Habits

> **Most of my advances were by mistake. You uncover what is when you get rid of what isn't.**
> ~ Richard Buckminster Fuller

Mistakes are great. When we make mistakes we learn and

grow! Mistakes help us build our risk muscle. Mistakes help us build self esteem, confidence and success. If you aren't making mistakes you won't be successful. In fact, if you aren't making mistakes, you are staying in the same place and playing it safe. Step up and make some mistakes. What are you waiting for?

In this section, I don't want to address any 'ol mistakes, I want to address repeated errors and mistakes. It's important for you to notice your repeated everyday mistakes, errors and other annoying habits such as -- forgetting to take the dry cleaning when you leave the house or losing your car keys on a regular basis. Maybe you always forget to call someone when you are expected to do so. What is this about? What's the story behind why you continue to make these errors? Why aren't you consciously paying attention to your actions? Are you sabotaging your success due to past unconscious behaviors? It could be any kind of mistake or forgetfulness. What is that "thing" you do -- over and over again?

"Katie", a sole entrepreneur, found herself in a pattern creating scheduling conflicts. We began to explore when this first started. Did it start before she began her business two years ago? She answered that she wasn't aware of it before because she just needed to show up at her place of work. After a few more questions we found that she had a pattern of not creating proper success habits when mistakes occur. Katie felt disappointed in herself when she made mistakes but she didn't take action to ensure they weren't repeated. She said she tries to leave the mistakes in the past. This seems like a great philosophy, doesn't it? There is a big difference between ignoring mistakes and putting actions in place to ensure they don't happen again.

Today, mistakes for Katie trigger her to pay attention and know that everyone makes mistakes. She has given up her self-disappointment and mental abuse. Mistakes trigger self-responsibility for Katie. She, now, takes action to create systems that ensure the same mistake won't happen twice.

Find YOUR Dragons: Daily Questioning

If things aren't working in your life, daily questions may help life flow with more ease.

Since we manifest on a daily basis it's important to check in with yourself and see how things are unfolding everyday. Daily goals are like little puzzle pieces in your big vision puzzle. Did one of your puzzle pieces fall into place today?

Dragon Diary Entry

If you see yourself making the same error or always seem stuck at the same time in a project, write it down in your journal. Awareness is the first step. These events offer you opportunities to explore the operating (dragon) behaviors and beliefs. Keep this dragon in your journal while you explore these retraining questions.

1. What can I do to ensure this doesn't happen again?

2. What can trigger me to consciously watch out for this repeating habit? An example could be as simply as consciously watching your hand put down the keys when you return to your home.

Here are a few questions to help you KNOW yourself better. Ask these questions everyday in search for limiting beliefs, mental patterns and even successful habits.

Daily Questions or "Ask List":

1. Am I enjoying each moment of my day?

What moments aren't full of joy? When you feel in love or in joy with something you are "on-purpose." The goal is to do more things you are aligned with and delegate the rest.

2. Do I love the compensation? This doesn't have to be a dollar amount, but you must feel that you aren't being taken-for-a-ride emotionally, physically, or spiritually.

3. If I don't enjoy it, why am I putting up with it? What is the obstacle (a.k.a. dragon) that is causing me to live this way? What can I do about it? Can I choose to feel differently about this?

DRAGON MASTERS
Make daily adjustments to get what they desire.

End-Of-Day Questions:

1. What felt good and worked well today?

2. What patterns did I see? Are these patterns beneficial to my future? Where did this pattern

come from? Can I replace this behavior with a different behavior?

3. Where did I get distracted? When did I feel I wasn't "on-purpose?" Did anything happen today that caused me to lose focus?

Rule #7:
Reset Your Mindset

Change Old Stories

One of my yoga teachers, Baron Baptiste, said, "It happens Now Here not Nowhere." At the time, I thought it was a little strange. Of course, I am here. Where else would I be? Until I realized I needed to answer ... "Is your mind Now Here?" Do you feel you're waiting for something better? Think about this for just a moment. How often do you think or obsess about the past or the future? Are you wondering what someone thought about you after your conversation? Or maybe your head is in the future thinking about your next meal or what you are going to write in an e- mail blast that goes out tomorrow.

Wait. Stop. It starts 'Now Here.'

You were born into this world with all the faith in the world that you would be taken care of. You knew all your needs would be met. You were present and curious about what events occurred during your day.

Life begins to change by the age of two. When you are told, "No, don't touch, don't put it in your mouth." You know the drill.

In the book, *The Four Agreements* by Don Miguel Ruiz, Don talks to us about "Breaking Old Agreements". He says, "Very young children are not afraid to express what they feel. They are so loving that if they perceive love, they melt in love. They are not afraid to love at all. This is the description of a normal human being."

Can you step back and remember the time when you were free and authentic like a child? Now is the time to let go of the fearful, limiting ideas, beliefs and lack of confidence, security or love that aren't aligned with your dreams and authentic self.

Leave everything in the past. Observe the mind and every time a thought comes up ask yourself, "Is this thought of past, present, or future?" How long (time yourself) can you keep your mind out of any past thoughts and future moments? The past is a mere memory and the future is a mere fantasy. This means that you need to deal with issues in the now. Redirect the mind into the present time. What do you experience and feel right now?

When you do find a dragon pattern, have no judgment, write down the situation in your journal and name your dragon. Keep him there until you have the time to open your journal and recreate thoughts to retrain your wild dragon. This chapter will help you train your wild beast.

> "Then you will know the truth, and the
> truth will set you free."
> John 8:31-33

Now that we have explored unconscious behaviors and mental dragon-like patterns, let's explore what lies deeper within so we can stop operating on these patterns.

Make a Strategic Plan for Dragon Training

STEP 1: Choose your dragons to train. Journal about your thoughts and patterns discovered from the previous exercises. Look at each possible dragon and name it if you haven't already.

STEP 2: Dissect the pattern and start to understand your individual stories. What do you find yourself thinking?

> **A cluster pattern or dragon**
> **(unconscious past pattern) =**
>
> **a life event (present) +**
> **a thought (conscious) or a previous engrained**
> **thought (subconscious) +**
> **a feeling (subconscious).**

Example Dragon called "Evening Eating Dragon":

Evening Eating Dragon = evening relaxation activities + "I think I'll eat to fill this time and comfort myself" + boredom or craving (feeling).

Note: This does not include the battling conflict in your head (i.e. King Dragon #1: Mental Incongruent Mindy Dragon). All that's needed is the identification of the dragon! Leave your conscious desire out for now. The goal is to train this dragon into a different kind of thought pattern.

STEP 3: Accept this dragon as a part of you. Visualize what he looks like. Host a dialog with him and analyze the root cause with what I call "Whying It." See Figure 1 to follow.

DRAGON MASTERS
Teach their dragon(s) in a loving, nurturing and empowering way!

This dialog usually brings up other past events that you haven't let go of. Write down whatever comes to your mind. Get emotionally involved with any past ideas or thoughts as they come up so you can release them from your mind. Then burn or destroy the dialog and let that go as you become fully present in the moment.

STEP 4: Begin the retraining process. Address the underlining belief to change core beliefs. I want to reintroduce these three questions. Please commit them to memory. Use them when you need to make a decision.

1. Is this what I desire?

2. Is this aligned with my future path? This question helps you know that you are respecting your future wish. Every "should" now turns into a "could".

3. Is this for the greater good?

STEP 5: Remind your dragon in a loving way, that you

are not looking at past and present results, but you are presently moving forward with your intention. This means to stop looking at your present results and to your dragon for direction. It doesn't mean stop being present. Your present results are results manifested from your past. Keep weekly measurable results to direct you along the way. Remind yourself to rate each dragon behavior on a behavior improvement scale of 1-10, with 1 being no improvement and 10 being a complete transformation of your dragon each week.

STEP 6: Focus on your desires not your dragon's desires. Remind yourself to stop looking for answers from your past belief patterns. In other words, if you only think you can make an additional $1000, you will only be able to make an additional $1000. If you want to make an additional $5000, go for it. Go for what you want, not what you think you can get.

STEP 7: Feel as if you already have what you desire in your life. If you want to be a best-selling author, feel as if you already are. If you want a BMW feel as if you already drive one.

STEP 8: Have faith and be persistent. Know that what you want is coming your way. Remember to listen for the inspired ideas and actions to take.

STEP 9: Practice. Retraining your dragon takes about 21–60 days to integrate a complete mindset shift. So you will need to set up reminders for example, tickler e-mails to yourself, sticky notes by your toothbrush, a rubber band on the wrist. Whatever it takes to remind yourself that you are practicing this integration. Mentally remind yourself to change your thoughts day and night.

In the case of the "Evening Eating Dragon" or a "Mental Incongruent Mindy Dragon"; the event (evening relaxation activities) begins with the trigger -- the thought to fill your unmet need. The need you are trying to fulfill in this case is comfort, self-love, and fulfillment. It is not about food. It is about feeling complete. So focus on changing the thought and automatic habit. Instead of "I want to comfort myself, I think I'll eat" change it to "I think I'll wrap up in a blanket and watch a movie to comfort myself," or maybe it's, "I'll go take a bath to comfort myself," or maybe it's, "I'll call my best friend to comfort myself." Every evening!

The practice part is the retraining component. You must practice this process until you believe it and know it is the truth.

Figure 1: **Whying Method: "Fear Of Success Dragon"**
1. Dialog

Example 1: Dragon: I fear public speaking.

You: Why?

Dragon: Because I feel and look nervous.

You: Why?

Dragon: Because I am not confident.

You: Why?

Dragon: Because I am unsure how to present my material.

You: Why?

Dragon: Because I am afraid.

Now you have come full circle. Review the dialog. What area needs to be addressed? That's right, "How can you become more confident?"

Example 2: Dragon: I fear success.

You: Why?

Dragon: I am afraid of being thought of as a "fraud"

You: Why?

Dragon: Because no one wants to work with a fraud <--- This is the fear, not "fear of success".

2. Question your dragon with a yes or no question.
Am I a fraud? <-- Now, you know this dragon is a Wanting-To-Be-Worthy Wilma Dragon. Please proceed, but if necessary you may need to take small steps and practice some of the Wilma Dragon techniques.

3. Answer yes or no, then proceed.

a. Yes? In this scenario, it may just mean you haven't mastered your trade yet and you need to seek more skills before you seek massive exposure.

b. No? Great, now you can tame your "Dragon". Proceed with Steps 4 and 5.

4. Thank your dragon for being a part of your past history, let him know you are ready to proceed to dragon retraining.

5. Replace the past pattern or thought with your new "true" thought.

6. Experience the new retrained dragon by engaging in a present activity that would have usually brought up the feeling. Observe your new feelings and practice this new behavior.

Rule #8:
Be Fabulous

> **"In the enlightened state, you still use your thinking mind when needed, but in a much more focused and effective way than before."**
> ~ Eckhart Tolle

LIVE FABULOUSLY – RIGHT NOW! When your mind is fresh and free of thoughts you can clearly hear divine and inspired ideas. When you feel fabulous, fantastic and celebrate where you are right now, you can't help but attract more of that same. Why? Because you only accept fabulous experiences into your life and you stop limiting your success. Think about it. What if you just start over – without past sob stories? Pause. Let this idea absorb. Start now. Celebrate life now. Feel fabulous and leave the past behind.

More importantly, when you are present in the moment and feeling great, you feel enlightenment, joy, empowerment, freedom, love, appreciation and peace, and your energy tinkles from your head to your toes -- you vibrate at a higher frequency. When you vibrate at a higher frequency you attract what you desire effortlessly without taking any action. Doors open, opportunities arrive and you feel fabulously on-fire! This feeling happens when you are focused on what you are doing right now with the intention of creating more fabulousness.

Dragon Diary Entry

Rate the below questions on a 1-10 scale with 1 being the lowest and 10 being the highest. Add these questions on your weekly "ASK list."

1. How often am I fabulous?
2. How often am I having fabulous experiences?
3. How often do I feel fabulously on-fire?
4. What do I put up with that isn't fabulous?
5. How often do I feel I lead a fabulous life?

(cont.)

Create an intention to improve these ratings. Mark this page in your dragon diary and put a reminder on your calendar to revisit these questions in a month.

"Just be present and enjoy now, was the mantra I sang in my head for months before I began to feel happier and more present on a regular basis. And when my inner attitude changed, my external life changed along with it."
~ Jen Blackert

Now stop. Take a breath. Drop into your body. Feel your body within. Notice your eyes reading these words. Stay focused on what you are doing now, as you curiously anticipate your next appropriate action to take. If you trip and fall, you don't evaluate why, you just get up and find the necessary bandages to care for yourself. No thoughts of "I'm such an idiot, I can't believe you didn't see the branch", or "I need to be more careful."

Do you see what I mean by being present? Now take a deep breath and read on.

Characteristics of being present:

1. Your senses are sharpened and alive.

2. You stop thinking and you start feeling both emotions and physical senses.

3. You give your full attention to your senses and you are aware of what you're taking in through your senses. For example, you choose what you want to believe and what you don't want to believe every moment.

4. You remain in integrity with what you say out loud and in your head.

5. You focus and concentrate on what is happening now.

6. You curiously anticipate the next appropriate action.

7. You have no worry, anxiety, or depression as these are all long-term effects of the mind.

Inner Fabulousness

I have taught many clients to feel at peace in their own skin. I offer these guidelines as an optional tool to help you feel fabulous on the inside.

The eight guidelines are from Patanjali's eight limb (or rules) of yoga. They include:

1. 10 ethical ways of being in harmony with yourself (Yamas). These help you operate more consciously and at peace in your body. The 10 ethical ways include non-violence, truthfulness, non-stealing, moderation, non-possessiveness, purity, contentment, discipline, study, and surrender.

2. 10 ethical ways of treating others (Niyamas). These help you operate in a peaceful, loving community. They include non-violence, truthfulness, non-stealing, moderation, non-possessiveness, purity, contentment, discipline, study, and surrender.

3. Yoga Practice (Asana) as you know it... a series of postures to keep your body healthy and strong. The physical practice teaches you how to accept your body as it is today. This only means you aren't rejecting a part of you.

4. Breathing practices (Pranayama). When we notice the natural rhythm in life like the breath, we feel more alive. Here are five steps to get you started with a breathing practice or pranayama.

Step 1: Start paying attention to your breath. Notice

the body as it breathes. Notice your chest, ribs, belly and lungs. Feel the breath moving inside the body. Feel the air moving in and out of the body. Feel as if you could flow and move like the breath. What would that feel like?

Step 2: Now, begin to change your breath. Move the breath from the upper chest to the belly. Move your belly when you breathe.

Step 3: Continue by making the inhalation and the exhalation the same length. You can explore a one-count breath in and out and then change the count to a two or three-count inhalation and exhalation.

Step 4: Next, you can slightly hold your breath at the end of the inhalation and at the end of the exhalation. This slight hold is when you count each breath. I have heard it called the breath inside the breath. For example, if you are counting 50 breaths you would finish the inhalation and then count '1' then exhale and continue after every inhalation count the next number until you reach 50.

Step 5: Lastly, holding the breath longer between the

inhalation and exhalation. Count the seconds between each breath. Why? Holding the breath calms the nervous system and clears the mind.

5. Internal attention (Pratyahara) instead of external sensory. Start using your five senses internally. What do you see, hear, taste, feel, and smell inside your body?

6. Focusing (Dharana) attention on one point. For example, having a vision and going for it.

7. Concentration (Dhyana) and sustaining awareness for extended periods of time.

8. Quieting the mind (Samadhi) so you can gain some inner perspective and clarity.

This practice is like training a wild dragon. A dragon master doesn't abuse their dragon, but demands focus and regimen. Your mind works the same way. It's a process in which you train, demand, and command your mind to obey you.

DRAGON MASTERS
Practice conscious presence daily

When you are present and feel fabulous inside and out, more energy is focused on the task currently at hand. You may feel you are igniting your fire and your conscious actions are amplified. You get the greatest bang for you buck, because you are aligned with your authentic energy. You are vibrating at a higher frequency and you attract what you are in alignment with faster.

Rule #9:
Have Faith

> "Mark 11:24 Therefore I tell you, whatever you ask for in prayer, BELIEVE that you have received it, and it will be yours."

Faith gives us the courage to make the conscious decision first without knowing all the details involved. Once you decide to do something, your mind is tuned into that solution and the universe conspires. But you must avoid any dragons telling you ... "You can't do that, you're not good enough." Or, "That will cost too much money." Or maybe it's, "That is too much work and I don't want to put forth the effort."

If you want something whether it's money, a thriving business, or a baby, you should never worry about whether or not you will receive it. You must make the decision to make it happen. This means you need to discard all possibilities of returning to what is safe and known. Fight for what you desire like a dragon would fight for his eggs. Dragons are patterns. Why not create a dragon in your mind that makes decisions and takes fearless action. Leave the exit strategy to the universe. Learn to replace any fear of failure with 100% faith.

> **"For the thing which I greatly feared is come upon me, and that which I was afraid of is come unto me."**
> *Job 3:25*

This is another example of the universal magnetic. If you fear something with your magnetic thoughts, you will attract what you fear. If you fear being poor then you will be poor. You manifested your thoughts, emotions, and feelings.

DRAGON MASTERS
Replace fear with faith.

Let's go back and revisit your future visions. Think of your vision as a chessboard. You don't know how the game will finish. You choose your next move when the time is right.

You will notice that the universe works the same why. It only reveals the choice or opportunity one step or two at a time. When you can't see all the moves, you may allow fear to creep in and change your actions. You can't see "how" to win the game or finish on top, so you become extremely cautious about what to make as your next move. Fear is a signal of danger upon what we perceive and often based on our imagination.

When fear creeps in, redirect your mind to knowing this is just a feeling and your vision is coming to you. It may not show up exactly as you envisioned it, but stay focused on your desires and they will come your way. Be fearless. The universe is always rigged in your favor!

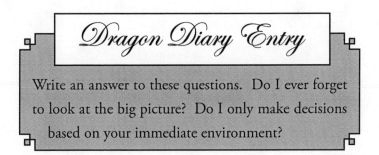

Dragon Diary Entry

Write an answer to these questions. Do I ever forget to look at the big picture? Do I only make decisions based on your immediate environment?

Rule #10:
Invoke Your Intuition

"The sixth sense probably is the medium of contact between the finite mind of man and Infinite Intelligence, and for this reason, it is a mixture of both the mental and the spiritual"
~ Napoleon Hill

Through daily prayer and meditation, I have become aware of how my five senses (touch, sight, smell, taste, hear) are used inside my body as well as on the outside of my body. Intuition is inner understanding that directs you to do what you ultimately need. It tunes your inner senses and offers a guide for how to know inspired thoughts. Intuition has helped me live a life with a greater sense of faith, presence, peace, purpose and flow.

Maybe you can relate to this kind of intuitive awareness.

- The voice in our head that says, "Help that stranger," "Look up! The cars are stopping in front of you," and "Take the back road." You will know when you hear these thoughts. They are clear, concise, and to the point.

- The feeling in your gut sometimes referred to as "gut instinct." Sometimes it can be felt as a lump in the throat and is thought of as the sixth sense.

- A subtle knowingness that seems like it may be from intellect, but you can tell it really isn't. You know it to be true even though you don't have factual information or you just feel inspired.

- Intuition shows up in consistent messages or signs. Have you ever thought about a topic and that same topic is found in an article or book you read the next day? This is a great indicator that you are aligned with the topic and you should make your next move.

When you use your intuition regularly, you live a life of ease and flow.

I have helped numerous clients understand the repetitive nature of their thoughts. Once they understand the repetitive thought, they are able to intuitively question themselves to learn what hidden benefits they obtain by keeping either the dysfunctional thought or pattern or the inspired thought at bay. This helps them learn the truth about the thought or pattern. Once the truth is revealed, new healthy behaviors (dragons) can be established.

"Jess", a yoga teacher, found that she continued to injure herself while teaching one particular class. I had her begin questioning herself. "Why did I choose to hurt myself?" After initially stating that she didn't choose to, we learned that she was getting attention from a student she had a crush on. This information came from her intuitive mind. It wasn't logical conscious thought. Although Jess wasn't intentionally injuring herself, we found that some part of her was benefiting from the injury.

Now, Jess can teach this class without self-injury. She also knows that if she likes this man, she can take healthy actions to pursue him.

Four Steps to Developing Intuition:

Step 1: Start by knowing you can develop your intuition and have faith. Your intuition will never steer you wrong. You are intuitive. It is a God-given gift.

172 | Seven Dragons

Step 2: The breath is the first action step to tapping into our inner being. Breath can touch many of the inner spaces of the body and allow you to begin to feel yourself internally.

Step 3: Clear all possible mental clutter by focusing on the breath from step 2. We have been offered so much external knowledge and information from the media that we have stopped listening to our gut instincts. We have stopped listening to our bodies. We have been offered so much external knowledge and information that we have stopped listening to our gut instincts.

Step 4: Test yourself! The next time the phone rings, see if you have an idea of who it before you check the caller ID or answer the phone. This is not predicting, this is simply having an idea of what is already true and present.

Be sure to create a journal entry on your experiences.

Intuition is a wonderful gift that allows us to see core truth, insight and guidance from our higher self. Some people believe this information is from their angels and spiritual guides. Intuition is the belief coming when you know that this direction is available to you and it can direct you to the truth.

Reminder

"The only thing some people do
is grow older."

~ Edgar Howe

By this point you understand how we are conditioned and programmed beings. You understand how to uncover hidden patterns and reprogram your mind to live the life of your dreams.

Here's Your Challenge:

I want to challenge you to raise your consciousness and continue to update your belief systems on a regular basis. I want to challenge you to act from your higher self. and express your personal and original thoughts everyday.

Have fun. Your adventure is just beginning.

Special Free Gift
from the Author

FREE
Test Drive Jen's Principles
Dragon Diary Membership

Receive ongoing advice!

Yes Jen, I want to take you up on your offer of a FREE Three-Month Dragon Diary Membership, which includes:

1. Jen's Attraction e-Newsletter
2. 40% discount on all products and classes
3. Monthly group coaching classes

There is a one time charge of $4.95 to cover administrative fees for three months of the FREE membership newsletter and you can cancel anytime. If you are interested, please email me at jen@jenblackert.com. If you would like to continue membership after 3 months, you will be charged $47 per month.

Jen's Coaching Company

The Think Big University provides training, coaching and consulting in the areas of:

> Mindset & The Law Of Attraction
> Emotional Eating Coaching
> Internet Marketing Training
> Author Marketing Training
> Keynotes & Workshops

Get free information by subscribing to Jen's Attraction Tips at www.jenblackert.com.

For support in implementing the Seven Dragon principles, receive personal coaching or join Jen's community at www.jenblackert.com.

Suggested Reading

Canfield, Jack. The Success Principles. New York: Harper-Collins, 2005.

Eker, T. Harv. Secrets of the Millionaire Mind. New York: Harper-Collins, 2005.

Hawkins, David R. Power vs. Force. California: Hay House, 1995.

Hill, Napoleon. Think and Grow Rich. New York: Ballantine Books, (reprint) 1999.

Leonard, Thomas J. The Portable Coach. New York: Scribner, 1998.

Miedaner, Talane. Coach Yourself To Success. Illinois: Contemporary Books, 2000.

Myss, Caroline. Sacred Contracts. New York: Harmony Books, 2001.

Schwartz, David J. The Magic Of Thinking Big. New York: Simon & Schuster, 1987

Weiss, Alan. Million Dollar Consulting. New York: McGraw-Hill, 1992,